Men in the Mirror

For Mark

Men in the Mirror

Men's Fashion, Masculinity and Consumer Society

Tim Edwards

CASSELL

For a catalogue of related titles in our
Sexual Politics/Global Issues list please write to us
at the address below.

Cassell
Wellington House
125 Strand
London WC2R 0BB

PO Box 605
Herndon
VA 20172

First published 1997

British Library Cataloguing-in-Publication Data
A catalogue record for this book is available from the British Library.

ISBN 0–304–33789–7 (hardback)
    0–304–33790–0 (paperback)

Designed and typeset by Ben Cracknell Studios
Printed and bound in Great Britain by Biddles Ltd
of Guildford and King's Lynn

Contents

Acknowledgements

This book, like many before and after it, was written predominantly in isolation. I have special reason, then, to be grateful for the support that I have been given during its production. Particular thanks are due first of all to the Department of Sociology at the University of Leicester, and particularly Sallie Westwood, for providing me with the opportunity and the support to complete the project. I would also especially like to thank my mother for her constant encouragement, Sam Ashenden for her enthusiasm, comments and the all-important shopping trips (!), and Colleen McLaughlin for keeping me sane. In addition, important thanks are also due to Kathryn Earle, Peter Howarth, Lawrence Michaels, Mary Spillane, Nick Sullivan, Justin Vaughan, the late Michael VerMeulen, and Elizabeth Wilson. Gratitude also goes to those anonymous reviewers who provided me, perhaps unintentionally, with the axes to grind. In the final instance, though, gratitude goes to Roz Hopkins at Cassell for her easy-going support and for putting it into print.

Preface

Of all motivations for this work, the one of personal interest was not the most significant. In fact, my key motivation was the question of social change. My primary inspiration lay in perceptions of the 1980s, a decade that not only witnessed the rise of Reaganomics and Thatcherism to world dominance, but simultaneously saw an apparent explosion in the production, and indeed consumption, of men's fashion. Central in this was the image of the infamous yuppie. The yuppie was not only a product of economic expansion in the financial sector, he was an advocate of the most striking conspicuous consumption since the Second World War, posing, parading and swaggering around the City in his pinstripe and power-look suits, ties and accessories, swinging his attaché case, talking animatedly on his mobile telephone, endlessly flicking the pages of his Filofax, slicking his hair and using every excuse to get into and out of his suit, his tie, his striped shirt and, of course, his Porsche.

His underclass counterparts were the rising ranks of working classes, students, drop-outs and the unemployed, who refused to wear suits yet adopted a uniform of 501s, trainers and 'Top Man meets the locker-room' fashions of sport couture, faked, copied and cut for those who could not afford the designer prices. These men displayed their clothes outside, on the 'scene', hanging around on high-street corners. Crucial in either case was the authenticity of 'the look', constructed through logo and label culture. Whether it was Armani or Nike, the product had personality and cult status.

Marketers seized upon the opportunity with dizzying speed and efficacy, flooding the market with old products wrapped up into a new 'lifestyle' miscellany and displayed in 'outlets' with the utmost cleverness: less was more. As if this were not enough, the same whirlpool whipped up new markets for new products for new men: moisturizers and accessories, a store full of ties, style magazines for guidance and mail-order directories for the hectic lifestyle. Advertisers seized on anxieties and desires for the new look–new man, and to top it off, pornography for women was expanded. For what the New Man was sold over and over and over again in the 1980s was himself and his sexiness: an auto-erotic sexiness of soft cotton Calvin Kleins under cool wool and worn-in denim, with a hint of silk and a splash of scent, a smoothing of cream and an invigorating rub-down in the shower afterwards when the sweat set in – for let us not forget his physique, oiled, muscled, pumping and ready for action in the boardroom or the bedroom.

Whether a crude marketing device, a turnaround in sexual politics, or a development in the very nature of masculinity itself, something was happening to menswear and something was happening to men. The important questions were how and why this was happening; whether it was really new; and, most sensitively, what the potential impact was.

Personal motivations do of course underpin my interest in these questions. I was always interested in my own appearance, spent time and money on it, desired new looks and, in particular, was enraptured with the power of clothes and accessories, or even simply colour itself, to transform mood, appearance and, ultimately, personality. It is this sense of mutation which lies at the centre of my interest in fashion and it ties in with a certain set of slightly more political assertions including the construction of artifice and androgyny. Although also a stereotype, this mutation is perhaps part of the appeal of fashion for women. And for gay men, the endless playing with appearances does start to undermine the essentialism of patriarchal masculinity. This also partly explains some men's resistance to fashion on the grounds of its effeminacy.

To put it personally, I recall strongly how my father felt undressed without a tie, his distress at odd cuts of suits, and his horror of pastel colours, whilst I started to play gleefully with the pieces of appearance like a child at Christmas. Similarly, I remember vividly the shock impact of Brut and Old Spice in the shops and the concerns of the tabloid press with footballers' blow-dryers. This showed up the same old rumblings of effeminacy, and exposed one of the great contradictions of fashion: for me it meant finding my own individuality, whilst for my father, and others, it was the means to conformity. Similarly, this had mixed implications at school, as whilst the rest of the class leapt into a uniform of Doctor Martens and Adidas sports, I started to look smart. This conformed to some of the institutional rules yet put cracks in the code of the class. This extended through to university where I routinely insisted on looking clean and well-cut when everyone else looked messy if not dirty. Coincidentally, it not only caused commotions with students, it concerned lecturers who felt I should conform to the casual iconography of the 1960s, echoing endless heated discussions with student friends where I protested that appearances were only appearances and not signs of voting patterns. Feminist friends were similarly divided as to whether heels, skirts and make-up were the tools of oppression in themselves or whether more opposition lay in challenging the male assumptions and reactions to them.

More particularly, as a graduate of the 1980s and a primary candidate for yuppie success, I felt a strong sense of unease as I sat in interviews and waiting rooms watching anxious interviewees in power-look suits and, more insidiously, selection panels adopting the same look and espousing values of salaries and leadership for which the clothes and the accessories were all too critical to success. I actually liked the look itself: I found it sharp, smart and sometimes sexy. But whilst I could, and later did, pull it all off for myself, the look was still only a look for me, and in the corporate world it was, in short, taken all too seriously. Later, when pornography for women came to include everything from strippers to postcard nudes, what impressed me was how this was rapidly transforming itself into the image of successful contemporary masculinity, to the point where, from Woolworth's to San Francisco, the same muscular look was presented as the most socially approved. This was also increasingly taken up in sports, locker rooms and multi-gyms where young men were trying to make themselves look the same. The key question again was why, how and with what impact we had come from the 1970s, where even pastels and antiperspirant were suspect, to the 1990s, where an iron-pumping narcissism is positively socially approved. Or, to put it more simply, what drove men into the mirror in the 1980s? These are, then, the key questions that drive the ensuing discussion.

Introduction:
Men in the Mirror

> Shyly, perhaps even fearfully, first because it is merely a man, because man has not meant to be 'seen', because it is the awesome and ineffable modern, and because it is only clothing, we must take a hard, masculine look (or, alternatively, a female's gaze) into the mirror and to reckon with men's fashion. (Chenoune, 1993, p. 5)

This is a book about fashion; it is also a book about masculinity and a book about consumer society. Most importantly, it is a book about all three. It is my primary assertion that the past ten to fifteen years have seen a resurgence of interest in the concept and practice of men's fashion. Academically, attention to fashion for men as opposed to fashion for women has also increased, particularly in the context of cultural and media studies of the New Man, although no single full-length sociological study of men's fashion yet exists.[1] This sociological neglect of fashion reflects the historical location of the study of fashion within the arts rather than within the social sciences, although the most cursory consideration of fashion demonstrates its sociological importance as an individual yet social, active yet structured, creative yet controlled phenomenon: in short, a perfect example of structure and action.[2]

Recent attention to men's fashion has raised many important questions concerning the nature and interpretation of contemporary images of masculinity, yet has often neglected wider sociological questions concerning the causes and outcomes of the phenomenon itself, often seeing the expansion of men's fashion as the simple outcome of developments in sexual politics or, more particularly, as a response to a crisis in contemporary masculinity (Chapman and Rutherford, 1988; Mort, 1986; Simpson, 1994). Consequently, I assert here that this expansion is more the outcome of wider developments in consumer society, and in particular marketing and advertising, and not simply a response to advances in feminism or predicaments concerning masculinity. Most importantly, I see masculinity as increasingly reconstructed as part of consumer society, as a matter of appearances and shopping practices or, to put it more simply, I perceive masculinity as increasingly premised more upon consumption than production. In addition, most controversially, I then consider these developments to be as equally personally destructive and socially divisive as they are individually expressive and democratically utopian. These are contentious statements or assertions to make and it is therefore not my intention to unpack them further in this introduction, rather to do so throughout the remainder of the text. It is, however, necessary to start with some definitions.

Defining fashion

Fashion is a multi-faceted concept. It refers simultaneously to dress, to design, and to style. As a result, we talk of what is in fashion, who is in fashion, and refer to fashion more actively as design itself, for example, in the phrase 'after a fashion'. Consequently, it is a uniquely diverse and ephemeral term that is profoundly difficult to define or pin down. In addition, confusion centres on the distinction of dress or clothing from fashion. Dress essentially refers to prevailing forms of personal decoration and adornment; whereas clothing rather more specifically applies to textiles or articles of dress *per se*; and fashion, in addition to this, focuses upon socially approved or desired styles of dress. Thus, clothing is part of dress and dress is part of fashion. Traditionally, though, discussion of fashion has tended to define it in limited terms of haute couture due, at least partly, to the location of the study of fashion within the confines of art and design. Fashion is defined here in its widest sense to include all aspects of style and dress: the high street as well as the catwalk, accessories as well as clothes, advertising and men's magazines as well as Savile Row or Armani, and Next in conjunction with haute couture. The focus is, however, on men's fashion, men's style and men's dress, all of which have a history of running a poor second to the study of women's fashion.

The Marginalization of men's fashion

Women are fashionable but men are not . . . Accordingly, the rhetoric of men's fashion takes the form of a set of denials that include the following propositions: that there is no men's fashion; that men dress for fit and comfort, rather than for style; that women dress men and buy clothes for men; that men who dress up are peculiar (one way or another); that men do not notice clothes; and that most men have not been duped into the endless pursuit of seasonal fads. (Craik, 1994, p. 176)

The study of men's fashion remains marginal, historically, to the comparative investigation of women's fashion and dress, with some exceptions (Byrde, 1979; Chenoune, 1993; Hollander, 1994; Laver, 1968, 1982; Martin and Koda, 1989). Much of this is explained as the result of a historical focus on haute couture, which did not include men's dress or appearance until comparatively recently; or via the development of the women's movement and feminist analyses focused on the importance of women's dress (Ash and Wilson, 1992; Ash and Wright, 1988; Craik, 1994; Evans and Thornton, 1989; Wilson, 1985). However, the greater explanation for this academic neglect of men's dress lies in the gendered development of fashion itself. Fashion for the past 150 years at least was, and often still is, seen as 'feminine' or 'not masculine', and therefore not connected to men. Ultimately, this has meant that men themselves are simply not 'in fashion', in any sense, and men's dress is seen to lie outside of fashion itself. There is a strong sense in which this is *non*sense, for men's clothes are produced and consumed in much the same way as women's; and men, as approximately 50 per cent of the population, constitute a major, if not majority, sector of the fashion and dress industries.

Nevertheless, fashion for men is rarely taken as seriously as fashion for women, and menswear is seen primarily in terms of utility – a perspective which cannot account for the specific forms and meanings of menswear. The main example of the utility of menswear, namely the suit, is as much a symbol of masculine sexuality in terms of broadening shoulders and chest and connecting larynx to crotch through collar and tie, as it is a practical (if historically uncomfortable) uniform of respectability. The predictable plethora of papers following the development and expansion of 'menswear', and the phenomenon of the New Man in the 1980s in particular, served to prove the point further in showing up the lack of previous attention to men's fashion and the inadequacies of many feminist and non-feminist analyses alike.[3] These included the crude equation of sexual misrepresentation with social or political oppression, and a historic lack of attention to detail and nuance in men's dress. It is a central intention of this book, then, to 'redress' this situation in providing a thorough-going investigation into the nature, consequences and causes of men's fashion, the production and consumption of men's dress, and an assessment of the impact and effects of previous and contemporary developments in menswear upon men themselves and upon society as a whole.

One of the strongest assertions of the following investigation, then, is that men's fashion is indeed something to take seriously in itself, and as a microcosm of the macrocosm of men, masculinity and society. The point, put most simply, is that it is perhaps not appropriately 'masculine' to take a serious interest in men's fashion let alone one's own appearance. Consequently, what the study of men's fashion represents, *par excellence*, is the persistence of gendered attitudes, gendered relations and gendered stereotypes concerning men, masculinity and their place in society. Interestingly, an interest in women's fashion is seen as slightly more appropriate given the overtones of heterosexuality. As a result, the constant slithering of the 'not masculine' into the 'effeminate' and therefore the 'homosexual' is particularly apparent. The equation of fashion with the feminine, with the not masculine, with the effeminate, as well as with the homosexual, remains a chain of socially constructed and perpetuated links that are decidedly difficult to overcome. Importantly, then, this text attempts to tackle these difficulties through providing an analysis of men's fashion that does indeed take it seriously in itself, and as part of sociology; and seeks to undermine some of these assumptions in seeing men's fashion not as an artistic, gay or even feminist minority interest, but rather as a significant link in the connections of masculinity and society, past and present.

Masculinity and consumer society

The text is, first and foremost, sociological, and the concept of masculinity used is essentially constructionist: it is assumed that there is no universal or natural foundation to masculinity and that our understandings of gender identity and meanings will necessarily vary from time to time and place to place, and that they are, in addition, contingent upon individual and social interpretation. Most importantly, the study of fashion often highlights the very artificial or constructed – as opposed to natural or essential – nature of masculinity itself, for in fashion, masculinity, like clothes and accessories, is put on, swapped around and played with, like costumes at a masquerade or in the theatre.

The use of the term consumer society refers to a series of social, economic and sometimes political developments that characterize contemporary or late capitalist society.[4] These include the increasing organization of society and societal institutions around consumption; the expansion in time and money spent on consumption activities, from leisure and sports to arts and shopping; the snowballing symbolic significance of goods in constructing individual identities and group practices; the increasing commodification and aestheticization of everyday life; and the rising significance of consumerism in the reconstruction of social divisions.[5] There is also some parallel of the notion of consumer society with the concept of postmodernity, often criticized for its diffuse and ephemeral qualities. It is, perhaps, conversely useful in this respect and serves a particular purpose here in capturing the changing and contradictory nature of fashion itself and society today as it ceases to be what it was but is uncertain of what it is to become. Because of this, the relationship of fashion to postmodernity and consumer society is a central one that forms the ultimate focus of this work. This contrasts with a focus on consumer culture, common to some contemporary analyses, a concept seen here as insufficiently connected to wider social, economic or political developments, as it usually implies some measure of cultural autonomy (Featherstone, 1991; Lury, 1996; Mort, 1996).

Summary of main themes and arguments

As already stated, men's fashion is a critically neglected area of academic study and, in particular, of sociology. Studies of men's dress, like most studies of fashion, have tended to locate themselves within the confines of design or art history.[6] Whilst these studies have provided excellent sources of reference for academics and the fashion industry alike, there are two particular difficulties: firstly, the lack of a more social, economic or political focus to the work has left the study of dress in an often free-floating state devoid of theory or explanation for its significance; and secondly, the haute couture focus of many of these works has led to an elitist stance and a neglect of high-street styles and cultures. Consequently, I assert in the first instance that men's fashion needs understanding sociologically.

Following on from this, I also assert that there has indeed been a demonstrable expansion of interest in the concept and practice of men's fashion since the mid-1980s. Empirically, this claim is supported via several important developments. Firstly, style magazines such as *GQ* and *Arena* have developed, aimed specifically at a style-conscious male readership, which now constitute a growth market at least in the UK, often following the example of some parts of Europe and North America. Secondly, there have been changing and increasingly sophisticated uses of advertising and marketing segmentation in relation to men's fashion, again tending to follow the lead of the United States. Thirdly, there has been an increasing use of images of masculinity to sell everything from toothpaste to Levi's jeans and even washing powder. Fourthly, the sexual objectification of men has increased in the media, in terms of film, drama and soap-opera sex appeal, where the importance of Hollywood is particularly apparent, and also in the recent phenomenon of male strippers and pornography for women. And lastly, the market for men's fashion itself in the widest sense has grown, in terms of the rise of designer or designer-influenced fashion from Armani to Next, and including increased expenditure on everything from moisturizers to suits and from sportswear to hair treatments. Most importantly, this also includes the development and rapid expansion of designer collections for men from international corporations like Calvin Klein or Versace to smaller-scale operations such as Prada or Dries Van Noten.

A similar expansion in academic attention to all aspects of men's fashion and appearances has accompanied these developments. A common explanation is to see the expansion in men's fashion itself as a response to developments in sexual politics or, more particularly, to a crisis in contemporary masculinity.[7] Empirically at least, this claim seems contentious, as there is little evidence to support the claim that men or masculinity are indeed in any kind of crisis; whilst theoretically there is clearly a quantum leap from the impact of feminism upon women's lives to large-scale or generalized changes in men or masculinity. In particular, much of this discussion has centred on the now notorious phenomenon of the New Man in the mid to late 1980s. Men, it was said – mostly in the media – were now, if not nurturing and caring, then certainly narcissistic and self-conscious, with shelves stocked with half the contents of the local chemist. Academics were clearly more sceptical, yet were often seduced into thinking that this must all mean something to do with sexual politics. But, empirically at least, these developments were limited to the same highly specific demographic group: namely affluent young men with few financial commitments, defined more by their incomes and lifestyles than by their political persuasions and sexual behaviours.[8]

It is perhaps more accurate, then, to see the expansion of interest in the concept and practice of men's fashion as more dependent upon developments in marketing, advertising and, most widely, consumer society. Tied up with this were changes in demography, economics and ideology, as more men now lived on their own or without children, had high incomes from working in the whirlpool of opportunities that opened up in the City or similar activities in the 1980s, and were equally drunk on an intoxicating liquor of ideological individualism via everything from Thatcherism and Reaganomics to TV advertising.

Finally, and most contentiously, the outcomes or implications of these developments are uncertain, yet concern is raised as to the nefarious effects of stereotypes of masculinity in creating personal anxieties and reinforcing social divisions according to age, class and sexual orientation. In addition, such divisions have gained added significance in the light of developments in the practice of shopping itself and the use and non-use of social policy (from VAT to the computerization of credit controls and the privatization of transportation) to perpetuate inequalities of access to consumption in a society which is increasingly centred upon consumption.[9]

Synopsis of contents and scope

The text has four particular areas of concern. Firstly, the nature and interpretation of the history of fashion itself and, within this, the importance and meanings of men's dress. Whilst it is accepted that this is a necessarily somewhat relativist task, an attempt is made to draw out central lines of continuity and change within men's apparel that also shape the nature, design and meanings of men's clothing and appearance in contemporary culture. Secondly, a more concrete analysis of the contemporary marketing of men's fashion is provided. This involves the study of advertising and retailing and particular attention is paid to the developments within menswear in the 1980s. This is used simultaneously to analyse how masculinity itself is not only socially constructed but bought, sold and marketed. Thirdly, attention is given to the centrality of the representation in men's fashion in the media and, in particular, the development of style magazines aimed primarily at a male readership. Importantly, the viewing relationship is considered critically as an interactive construct that invokes contested definitions of gender identity and (most importantly) its relationship to sexuality.[10] Fourthly, and finally, the politics of fashion for men are considered primarily in terms of gender, class, race and sexuality. On top of this, though, an analysis is provided of the social policy affecting the consumption of men's fashion in a study of credit control, surveillance and shopping culture. It is argued that, in the final instance, this is the site in which social, economic and political inequalities are now increasingly located. The conclusion, then, ultimately provides an attempt to reconnect these four areas of concern, spread across eight chapters, in an analysis of the inter-relationships of fashion, masculinity and consumer society.

As a result, the chapters are ordered logically and progressively, unpacking the key arguments of the text in turn. Chapter One provides a commentary on the history of men's fashion itself and a critical analysis of costume history from the fourteenth century to the present day. It also gives detailed attention to the history of the suit. Chapter Two is a critique of classical historical, economic and psychological perspectives taken to explain the history and development of men's fashion, whilst Chapter Three is an investigation of more contemporary perspectives on men's fashion and, in particular, the phenomenon of the New Man. Primary attention is also given to Levi's advertising campaigns in the 1980s. Chapter Four provides an analysis of the marketing of men's fashion as the marketing of masculinity itself and how factors such as age, class, race and sexual orientation affect the consumption of men's fashion. It also includes a detailed study of the impact of the Next chain of stores in the 1980s and the importance of market segmentation and lifestyle advertising in men's fashion. Chapter Five gives a critical examination of the significance of men's style magazines such as *GQ* and *Esquire*, including content analyses of the magazines themselves and the results of interviews with some of their editors. Chapter Six offers an analysis of historical and contemporary developments in shopping, including department stores, shopping malls and mail order, as well as investigation into the complexities of its lived experience. Chapter Seven gives a critique of feminist, gay/lesbian and anti-racist perspectives on dress, appearance and fashion, as well as an analysis of subcultural theory and the links between men's fashion and popular music. Specific attention is also paid to the importance of vogue, drag and camp cultures. In Chapter Eight, an analysis of social policy is applied to the consumption of men's fashion and consumer society. It is asserted that this is now the central site for the reconstruction of racial, sexual and gendered as well as economic inequalities. Finally, in the Conclusion, it is pointed out that there are elements of change as well as continuity in the increasing construction of men as consumers of men's fashion and, indeed, masculinity.

Notes

1. See Ash, 1989; Barthel, 1992; Craik, 1994; Dyer, 1989; Mort, 1986, 1988; Nixon, 1992, 1993; Scheuring, 1988; Simpson, 1994; Spencer, 1992.

2. Structure and action, and their associated tensions, are concepts well known to any sociologist and refer to the theory of determination or, to put it more simply, to the extent to which society as a whole, or any part of it, is the outcome of individual actions in creating social structures or the result of social structures that control and constrain those actions. In relation to fashion, then, a key question is whether we dress to express ourselves and our individuality or even to create conventions, or whether we dress simply to conform and fit in to society in choosing from a predetermined set of items.

3. See particularly Mort, 1988; Nixon, 1992; Spencer, 1992.

4. Late capitalism is a concept used in some social theorists' work to outline a new point or level in capitalist societal development (see Giddens, 1990; Featherstone, 1991; Jameson, 1984, 1988).

5. These are all developments open to question, particularly in relation to their sometimes uneven and spasmodic impact. The commodification and aestheticization of everyday life refers to the expansion of monetary exchange and the importance of the *image* in everything from health plans to university degrees.

6. There is some considerable variation here but see: Batterberry and Batterberry, 1982; Byrde, 1979; Glynn, 1978; Hollander, 1988; Laver, 1968, 1982; Roach and Eicher, 1965; Yarwood, 1992.

7. See particularly Cook, 1994; Mort, 1986, 1988; Nixon, 1992, 1993; Simpson, 1994.

8. For an important collection on the theme of the New Man with varying interpretations, see Chapman and Rutherford, 1988.

9. For a path-breaking account of consumer social policy, see Cahill, 1994.

10. For an unpacking of the gender implications of the viewer–viewee relationship see particularly: Dyer, 1989, 1992, 1993; Gaines, 1986; Mulvey, 1975; Neale, 1982, 1983; Pumphrey, 1989; Rodowick, 1982.

His Story of Fashion

It is my primary intention in this chapter to try to explain and explore the often dual nature of the history and interpretation of fashion. There are essentially three sections: firstly, a discussion of the interpretation of fashion; secondly, an intentionally contrived consideration of the history of men's fashion more particularly; and thirdly, a detailed discussion of the history and indeed sexuality of the suit.

Fashion interpretation

> Writings on fashion, other than the purely descriptive, have found it hard to pin down the elusive double bluffs, the infinite regress in the mirror of the meanings of fashion. (Wilson, 1985, p. 10)

Fashion is often seen as a modern phenomenon, entirely dependent upon nineteenth- and twentieth-century capitalism for its development. Most historians of fashion are at pains to point out, though, that fashion, at least in the sense of style and design, has a very long history. They often take the rise of the market and mercantile trade in the sixteenth and seventeenth centuries as their starting point (Wilson, 1985; Yarwood, 1992). However, much depends on definition, and fashion – in the sense of mass production of goods for adornment – is indeed a more modern phenomenon, tied to the twin developments of industrialism and capitalism. More importantly, throughout time people have needed to cover themselves in textiles or skins to keep warm and, moreover, have sought to use dress as an indicator of social status or rank, personality or identity (Barnes and Eicher, 1992; Eicher, 1995; Roach and Eicher, 1965).

As societies have developed in complexity, populations have expanded, and multiple technologies for producing an increasing variety of clothing and physical adornment have been discovered, so the meanings attached to dress have also increased in their complexity and significance. Consequently, it is difficult to say with any degree of certainty today what any item of clothing or adornment actually means. For example, a man's suit, supposedly an indicator of the most extreme uniformity, conveys very differing meanings in different contexts and to different people. Cary Grant or Clark Gable dressed in a lounge suit signifies glamour and sexuality; whilst a similar suit on John Major suggests diligence, honesty and downright anti-sexual conservatism, whilst salesmen in suits attempt to convey equal amounts of sexuality and honesty. As a result, this makes the compilation and interpretation of any costume history extremely complex and uncertain.

In addition, this process works on several levels: firstly, there is the issue of finding data – and the further one travels in time and space, the more and more specious and spurious the data are. Secondly, when data are found, there is the fiendish difficulty of interpreting them and deciding what (if any) relationship 'what they might mean now or here' has to 'what they meant then or there'. Thirdly, all of this is then individualized as any one person reinterprets, re-presents or even reinvents the dress itself or its significance. Consequently, it is quite clear that there is no one history of fashion, that there is no 'essential' series of 'facts', no 'truth' and that all historical investigation is primarily a matter of interpretation. Importantly then, there are histor*ies* of fashion, or a series of reconstructed discourses resulting from intensive deconstruction of previous narratives of fashion.

This intense relativism does have its pitfalls, however, for it is quite clear that some interpretations are simply incorrect or unlikely, whilst others are more widely accepted and understood. To interpret a pair of men's jeans as an example of aristocratic effeminacy may not be impossible but is decidedly improbable. It is, perhaps, possible to relabel this in saying that there are both dominant and subordinate interpretations, and this point is explored further in Chapter Three.

Costume histories

The history of fashion was, and to some extent still is, most simply the history of costume. This comes primarily from the location of fashion as a discipline within departments of art and design and not departments of history and sociology. This is explained easily as the outcome of the importance of production to fashion or, to put it more simply, students of fashion tend to produce it as well as study it. This then opens up a gap for a more social or historical perspective on fashion and sets up a tension of what one might call critical, textual or traditional accounts of the fashion *garment* and more social, economic or historical perspectives on the fashion *phenomenon*.[1]

Importantly, the history of the study of fashion itself clearly gives greater significance to art and design, as more social, psychological and economic approaches are comparatively more recent. In particular, Elizabeth Wilson's *Adorned in Dreams*, published in 1985, still stands out as a forerunning *sociological* as well as feminist account of fashion. In addition, despite later examples of feminist, cultural or more specific perspectives upon fashion, the more socially oriented study of fashion has tended to collapse into articles and collections of its own (see Ash and Wilson, 1992; Ash and Wright, 1988; Craik, 1994; Evans and Thornton, 1989; Kidwell and Steele, 1989; Solomon, 1985).

Art and design perspectives on the development and history of fashion tend to take one of two forms: technical costume histories detailing dress through the centuries; or slightly more general perspectives which take a more social, though very simplistic, view of fashion as a 'reflection' of society.[2] The value of either perspective lies in the archival work and expertise involved as well as the provision of a series of reference works which are then open to multiple interpretation. It is difficult to see how a student of fashion could conduct any in-depth study without recourse to such works. What these artistically focused works also show, though, is a certain passion for their subject, a reverence, almost, for the details of dress, colour, fabric and texture. This is often linked to criticism of more social scientific perspectives as being insufficiently about the clothes themselves. There is some truth in this, particularly in the case of more politically driven analyses which have often sought to create overly convenient categories of dress. The clear difficulty at the end of the day, though, is the tension of drawing sufficient attention to the details of dress itself without missing out on its more social significance, and vice versa.

The equally clear difficulties in art and design perspectives, however, lie in the deep void of theory involved and, in particular, the presentation of fashion as 'facts' and not fiction or interpretation. A second and more political difficulty lies in the usually high degree of attention paid to haute couture and the neglect of more common dress. As haute couture was often only worn, or afforded, in highly aristocratic circles, this produces a rather distorted perspective, as it does not represent the dress of a group or society in its entirety. A third difficulty, specifically related to the latter approach, is the structural–functional notion that fashion simply reflects society, when equally one could say that fashion leads on to, or at least interacts with, wider aspects of society, particularly in practice and design as opposed to theory. At the end of the day, then, it is necessary to reconsider rather than ignore the 'facts' of fashion and costume history and represent these in a way which shows awareness of their relativity.

Costume dramas

Despite the importance of interpretation, there is still a sense in which fashion has a history. What we wear in the late twentieth century, we could not have worn previously, as it was not yet invented or discovered. We do not generally choose to dress in what we did then as opposed to what we do now. What follows, therefore, is an intentionally 'stagy' attempt to document the main, more concrete, developments in European men's fashion and dress. A secondary intention is to show how, in a sense, masculinity is performed *through* fashion – or how men's dress only makes sense when it is worn. There is no intrinsic masculine essence to men's clothes; they develop masculine meanings and associations when worn upon the male physical form or when men perform in them. It *is* my intention, then, to provide an informed starting place for the discussion of the development of men's fashion; it is *not* my intention to provide a definitive guide. End of prologue . . .

Act One: Medieval and Renaissance Men

Scene One (1410): Enter Prince Hall dressed in tunic, mantle and tights. The fabrics are fairly coarse and wool-derived, colours are earthy and the cut simple, providing a relatively natural silhouette, though the mantle is decorated with fur and widens his shoulders. His shoes are simple, flat and pointed, whilst he is clean shaven and his hair is fairly long and cut plainly in a straight line. He also wears a soft, though largish, hat.

Scene Two (1525): Henry VIII is dressed in doublet and hose, off-set by a large hat with many feathered plumes and a chamarre, or cloak, half covering the rest of his clothes. His doublet is elaborately trimmed with silks imported from Spain and slashes showing his shirt underneath. The colours are rich and strong whilst he sports an immense cod-piece upon his crotch. His hair is full, though not overly long and he has a short goatee. As the century progresses, his shirt collars grow higher and ruffs are introduced.

Scene Three (1645): Enter D'Artagnan waving a sword, with long and curling hair flying and ruff now falling. His cuffs are fancy and his gloves are long, off-setting his hat with a single plume. He sports a silk sash upon his exceptionally elaborate doublet and breeches worn with knee-high boots and a sumptuous velvet cape. He has a small, upturned moustache and pointed beard to add to the whole swashbuckling impact. Backstage: a Puritan man passes by, plainly dressed with a tall, hard hat, murmuring something about the pleasures of the devil.

Act Two: Romantic Masculinity and Industrial Man

Scene Four (1680): Louis XIV sits with his legs crossed, dressed in the utmost finery of silks, velvets and lace. His face is covered in white powder and he sports a beauty spot upon his cheek. His coat is finely decorated with silk ribbon and matches the cloth of his breeches to make a suit, whilst his waistcoat marks a colourful contrast. His stockings are of silk and his shoes too are decorated. Of most consequence is the immense wig he wears upon his head, off-set with a tricorne hat, while the room is filled with the scent of his latest fragrance.

Scene Five (1800): Mr Darcy dashes in displaying the new pantaloons, simply cut and neutral in colour, they are soft and closely fitting. His waistcoat is near white, contrasting with the strong blue of his tail-coat which makes him look most slim-waisted, whilst his hair falls forward in curls to his cravat. He is never seen without his black top hat, walking cane and cow-hide gloves.

Scene Six (1900): Victor or, on occasions, Victoria sports a top hat, spats and tails in the smartest black and white for evening wear, whilst his hair is short with whiskers. When outside, he wears an overcoat and carries a cane, now noticing some of his lower-class contemporaries are starting to wear the new style three-piece suit in a worsted material with a stiff-collared shirt and narrow tie.

Act Three: The Twentieth Century and Postmodernity

Scene Seven (1925): The Prince of Wales is seen sporting an entirely new garment, a sweater of Fair Isle wool which he couples with widely cut trousers in a soft woollen material commonly called flannel, ideal for weekend and country wear outside of the office and the City.

Scene Eight (1940): Cary Grant is on view wearing a new, smooth lounge suit cut with a wide silhouette that heightens his stature, whilst the low 'V' cut of his jacket displays a crisp white shirt and a most decorative silk tie. His shoes are highly polished and his hair is kept short, whilst he views the countryside from his new motor car.

Scene Nine (1960s/1970s): Enter a mod, a rocker and a punk causing great consternation with their loudness and outrage. The rocker has reinvented the frock coat into a long jacket with a velvet collar that covers very tight trousers and a shirt with a string tie. He has grown long sideburns and combed his hair into an immense quiff. The mod, meanwhile, wears a dark and narrowly cut suit with a black tie, whilst his short hair is oiled to the point of hardness. The punk snarls at all of this and pulls at the safety-pin he put through his ripped drain-pipe jeans and jerks at another attached to his leather jacket. His hair sticks up in nine-inch spikes of yellow and orange.

Scene Ten (1980s/1990s): A man passes by in a pin-stripe double-breasted suit with a bright silk tie, talking into a mobile telephone and carrying a personal organizer, when another young man strides in wearing a tight white T-shirt and snugly fitting and well-worn jeans. His hair is short though a shock of locks catches his eye. He stands centre-stage and tears off his T-shirt to reveal his golden smooth and muscled torso. Not content to stop there, he then proceeds to open his jeans, painstakingly slowly, button by button, for all to see . . .

Critical review

> There has been an affinity between the fashions of the sexes but at no time since the development of tailoring in the fourteenth century have their clothes been completely identical or interchangeable; sex has almost always been clearly differentiated by clothing. (Byrde, 1979, p. 11)

Despite the artificiality of the preceding description, it is important to try and discern and delineate some of the most important points concerning the development of men's fashion and dress. These fall roughly into five areas of concern.

Firstly, at least in western culture, men's dress is and always was different to women's. This may well seem a statement of common sense, yet it makes the vitally important point that fashion and dress have performed a more or less universal function of reinforcing gender difference. Whilst the form, content and meaning of costume have varied enormously, its overt sexing of the species has not. It is particularly important to note that as the complexities of dress and tailoring have increased and advanced, so the gendered differences in dress have often inversely increased in rigidity (Craik, 1994; Finkelstein, 1991; Hollander, 1994). In pre-mercantile times, in developing societies and in some non-western societies today, the gendered differences in dress are often far less pronounced: for example, in some African and Asian cultures as well as early ethnic groups, in Greco-Roman culture and, on top of this, in prehistoric times when simple tunics, cloaks or skins were worn (Barnes and Eicher, 1992; Eicher, 1995).

The role of dress in defining the genders is most evident, then, in modern western society and particularly in the case of children who are assigned to differing genders through their dress very early on and are 'dressed for sex' almost *ab ovo*: blue for a boy, pink for a girl; trousers for boys and skirts for girls. This progresses further into adulthood when dress is often used to heighten anatomical maleness in widening shoulders and chests, or to emphasize gender difference in defining legs, thighs or crotch areas. The contemporary development of the apparently gender neutral pair of jeans is an excellent example of how even the same item of clothing is used to add to gender difference through its fit alone. Nothing makes a man look more like a man than a pair of snug-fitting western jeans.

Secondly, changes and developments in men's costume and dress are traditionally and historically slower and fewer than those related to women. This is an important point, but is easily over-stressed. Whilst it is true that fashion cycles and changes in overall form were, and to a lesser extent still are, faster for women than for men, the more muted changes in decoration, detail and nuance are far more similar for each of the sexes. It is also worth pointing out that the overall form of dress since the rise of mercantile capitalism and trade has altered little for either sex, at least until the twentieth century. Men have always worn some variation on a coat or jacket, with or without a waistcoat, covering some sort of shirt and worn with either hose, breeches or trousers. They have worn, and some still do, tunics or robes, but have never worn dresses or skirts apart from ceremonial dress or perhaps the kilt, which remains more a national tradition than a fashion. High fashion's recent flirtations with the men-in-skirts theme – for example, Gaultier's designs in 1984 and Westwood's collections in the early 1990s – have remained minority concerns that have never, as yet, hit the high street.

Similarly women, in western society at least, have always worn some variation on the skirt and dress theme with some form of coat for further warmth. Women in trousers, at least without tunics that cover the top, did not appear until the twentieth century, very much spurred on through their roles in 'men's work'. Quite why this is so is uncertain, but the significance of women's roles in reproduction and child rearing and men's roles in production and work would seem to have something to do with it, as skirts have traditionally facilitated sexual and reproductive access and trousers have tended to develop as part of more sporting or active lifestyles. What is more, in this sense, dress for women has actually changed *less* than it has for men.

Most of the major changes in men's dress such as the development of the modern suit were often technologically driven, via developments in tailoring and the invention of the sewing machine, which Singer patented in 1851. This does not account though, as we shall see in the next section, for the specific form or meaning that men's dress takes, and less still for the variety of decoration, detail and nuance that has always added to its complexity.

Thirdly, and more controversially, there is a certain oscillation or tension in men's dress over the centuries which I shall call 'playboy' and 'puritan' tendencies.[3] These tendencies have coexisted in the past and continue to do so in the present, yet there is an added tendency for one or the other to gain ascendancy at a specific time or place. The fancy and decorous dress of the aristocracy in the early seventeenth century under the influence of France and Louis XIV is a clear case of more narcissistic and playboy-like influences, in turn echoing the grandiose extravagance of the Renaissance, and repeated in the romanticism of the turn of the nineteenth century; whilst the dour and industrially driven suits of the late nineteenth century echo prior medieval and Puritan factors that carry through to commerce in contemporary society, though often coupled with a more colourful and playful approach. It is important to add that the original Puritan dress of the seventeenth century developed as an opposition to the perceived extravagance of styles from Spain and France earlier on and has coexisted with this ever since. It is also interesting to note potential ways in which such changes intersect with the nature and position of men and masculinities. It is, perhaps, no coincidence that the rise of more formal or work-related dress in the 1980s occurred under the auspices of aspirational Thatcherism, recession and unemployment. These are very complex questions, though, to which I shall return later.

Fourthly, men's dress has a strong history of association with status or rank in society.[4] This not only applies to specialist, professional or spiritual roles and uniforms, but to the overall significance of class and work in men's lives. The lavish costumes of royalty in the fifteenth, sixteenth and seventeenth centuries were transferred into complex hierarchies of tailoring from the eighteenth century onwards. This still exists now in the minutiae of detail that accompanies formal dress, which can demonstrate status through the level of expense involved, and is often intricately tied to work roles where the rules of the right suit, knot in the tie and design of the collar are more rigid than the tightest corset.[5]

This has often led to the idea that men's dress is interlinked with the notion of utility and its purpose is practical rather than decorative. As we have already seen, this is qualified on several counts. In the first instance, men's dress has very complex meanings and even the most stoic of uniforms is on occasions transformed into decoration and intense sexiness in certain contexts including, for example, the strong sense of glamour and eroticism associated with American GIs dressed in their crispest uniforms. More importantly, the history of men's fashion has always shown significant attention to decoration and adornment for its own sake, though this is often juxtaposed with a more puritanical or conservative sense of status and tradition. It is also uncertain whether many of the actual forms of men's dress are indeed practical or convenient, as they often tie up the male anatomy in a myriad of fastenings and padding that restricts movement, is easily soiled, or is simply uncomfortable. This more problematic aspect of men's dress in fact leads on to the final point.

Fifthly, and finally then, men's dress has shown its greatest advances during the twentieth century and particularly in moves towards increased casualness and informality in attire that is, indeed, of more comfort and use. The rise of sweaters, shirts with fixed collars in softer materials, and a whole array of more casual trousers and jeans, as well as the widening influence of sportswear, has created a near revolution in men's clothing. Much of this development was driven by the invention and mass production of synthetic materials after the Second World War, and even by the zipper, which in the 1920s started to revolutionize the way men held up their trousers, did up their coats and even went to the lavatory! These changes have also affected women's clothes, but the effect on men, whose history of dress was effectively 'stuck' until after the Second World War, is perhaps more awe-inspiring. Men have only very recently experienced the range of formal and informal, coloured and varied choices that have presented themselves to at least more middle-class women for centuries, with all that entails in terms of freedom, personal expression and etiquette. It is also still the case that men's dress remains far more limited in form, style and design than women's dress. The rigidity of work and leisure expectations, let alone questions of looking 'masculine', still remains, as a suit and tie, for example, is still the only socially approved office and City attire, whilst chinos or jeans with an open-necked shirt and casual jacket remains a near uniform for the weekend.

Perhaps more importantly, the development of more casual attire for men with its accompanying rhetoric reflects the increasing influence of North American culture upon clothing through the twentieth century. Whilst Europe, and Spain and Italy in particular, dominated design in medieval and Renaissance dress, and the fashion houses of Paris and Milan, as well as the sartorial and street figures of England, from Armani to Hamnett and Dior to Westwood, still dominate much of haute couture, the rise of the USA in manufacturing and designing casual wear from sportswear to denim, as well as haute couture at the level of Calvin Klein and Ralph Lauren, is of profound significance. Calvin Klein's name, in particular, is now almost synonymous with designer casual wear as well as the colossally successful fragrance collections.

This is of particular importance to menswear, where much opposition to casual wear came from its associations of effeminacy in comparison with more formal wear; a sweater did not invoke the same masculine sexuality or power as a collar and tie. Importantly, then, the physically self-conscious and sporting looks of trainers and western jeans, for example, revolutionized the means through which men could still look like men without a suit and tie. These are points I will explore in later chapters. To start to sum up the present one, I wish to present a detailed study of the history and sexuality of the suit.

The history and sexuality of the suit

> Although male heads of state wear suits at summit meetings, male job applicants wear them to interviews, and men accused of rape and murder wear them in court to help their chances of acquittal, the pants-jacket-shirt-and-tie costume, formal or informal, is often called boring or worse. Like other excellent and simple things we cannot do without, men's suits have lately acquired an irksome esthetic flavor, I would say an irritating *perfection*. (Hollander, 1994, p. 3)

The suit is often seen as a uniform in itself and as a uniform phenomenon. Its primary origin, most historians of fashion point out, lies in the late seventeenth century when, under the influence of French fashion, the three-piece outfit of coat, waistcoat and breeches became commonplace (see Amies, 1994; Hollander, 1994; Laver, 1968, 1982). It is important to point out immediately that this set of clothes was not only a far cry in terms of design from the industrial and commercial suits of the nineteenth and twentieth centuries, it was also a very far cry in terms of meaning. The seventeenth-century suit was a highly ornate outfit with strong associations of aristocratic expense and effeminacy, as the working classes were still often confined to coarse worsted or occasionally cotton outfits often without decoration, whilst some middle- and particularly upper-class men commonly wore wigs and powder and decorated their outfits amply with ribbon. Indeed, both Hollander and Finkelstein see the classicism of the turn of the nineteenth century as critical in starting to set up the austerity of design in menswear that has often followed since (Finkelstein, 1991; Hollander, 1994).

Earlier, during the eighteenth century, the suit had become only gradually simpler and more refined, although the invention of the spinning jenny in 1764 made wider production of finer textiles a lot easier. There was, interestingly, much conflict concerning the introduction of pantaloons, which were seen initially as unaristocratic and so were resisted in the upper classes, though their practicality appealed increasingly to other classes and therefore the aristocracy eventually capitulated (see Yarwood, 1992). Styles were increasingly simplified with fewer fastenings and adornments and more muted colours, particularly for the less affluent. In contrast with contemporary associations, strong and colourful effects were associated with the upper classes who could afford the more expensive dyes and imports. Purple was the most expensive and was therefore adopted in the High Church and by royalty. This quite clearly has a very different resonance to today's associations of loud colours with the 'cheap' and 'trashy', an idea developed partly from the turn of the twentieth century onwards, when gaudy colours were identified with prostitution. The contrast of the colourful world of Jane Austen's quasi-aristocratic heroes such as Mr Darcy with the Dickensian working-class dreariness of David Copperfield and Oliver Twist is a case in point, and is often cited as a prime example of the move towards more austere modernity in the design of menswear (Finkelstein, 1991; Hollander, 1994; Wilson, 1985). What Flügel called the Great Masculine Renunciation in *The Psychology of Clothes* encapsulates well this strong sense of a unilinear shift in men's dress from finery and decoration to simplicity and austerity yet, as we shall see, it is often empirically limited if not entirely incorrect (Flügel, 1930).

It is often pointed out, for example, that the rise of the dull grey suit of contemporary society coincided with the rise of industrialization (Amies, 1994; Craik, 1994; Laver, 1968). But the development of the dark modern suit for commerce did not start until well into the Victorian era. Indeed, it was not until the 1880s and 1890s that the stoic uniform of commerce really took off and, even then, the smartness of evening dress in top hat and spats also reached its peak of popularity. Interestingly, at the same point, the sporting influence upon men's fashion became more apparent as the cut of the single-breasted jacket, curving from the waist down, crossed over into work and casual wear from its origins as a riding coat. In conjunction with this, the double-breasted style spread, from more naval or 'reefer' jackets in tandem with the aptly named blazer derived likewise from the brightly coloured sports coat, or 'sports jacket', as a smart and sometimes dashing alternative adornment. Dinner and smoking jackets, often in plush velvet of deep crimson or emerald green, were also introduced at the same time, as were a variety of suitings for different functions such as the tweed walking suit, the Norfolk hunting jacket and the seaside stripes. Whatever apparent uniformity existed in the development of the modern suit was soon undermined and essentially confined to City commerce, though even this was livened up in the use of pinstripes. It is important to point out, then, that whatever the suit was, it was not a uniform phenomenon.

Much of the insistence upon men's apparent confinement to the uniform of the suit centres on its contrast with the rapid developments in women's fashion at the time. Styles for women around the turn of the century were increasingly softened and de-corseted, particularly in the designs of Charles Worth and Paul Poiret. This development rapidly accelerated after the Second World War with the highly influential New Look of Christian Dior which sought to provide a feminine and affluent contrast of falling neck lines, flowing skirts and floods of chiffon to the Utility Look of the *woman*'s suit, which was perceived as much more 'masculine', though later completely reinvented in style and meaning through the phenomenal influence of Coco Chanel. On top of this came the flapper era of straight line simplicity – and all of this in the space of thirty or so years.

The increasing variety of styles of women's dress, and their colourfulness and comfort on occasions, formed the focus of opposition for the Men's Dress Reform Party in the 1930s. The Party was set up in 1929 to shake up what was perceived as the increasing dullness, formality and discomfort of men's clothes. Not surprisingly, the suit, and particularly the stiff collar and tie, came under particular attack. Consequently, the Party was often quite successful in at least questioning the naturalness or normality of some of men's dress. It was less successful, however, in constructing alternatives, particularly to the suit, often coming up with floppy and poorly executed ideas that reworked the open collar and shorts styles already popular in sports and adolescent cultures.

The collapse of the Men's Dress Reform Party in 1937 signposted many of the developments to come in men's dress, including the move towards increased casual wear. However, it also highlighted the strength of convention still evident in men's dress, particularly where work was concerned, and perhaps more importantly the impasse in surpassing the suit as the perfect outfit for any meaningful or formal function. It also exposed the suit's associations of intense masculinity, of grown-up-ness, and indeed of manhood (see Burman and Leventon, 1987).

Meanwhile, men were still confined to black, white and grey, grey suits: or were they? Whilst it is true that dress for men changed little until after the Second World War, there was much increasing diversity around function and detail, as already mentioned. In addition, the lounge suit was introduced as a contrast to the work suit, without the waistcoat to protect the shirt and create further warmth. The lounge suit was precisely 'a suit for the lounge', for gentlemen to 'lounge' in and still look appropriately dressed up to entertain guests. It is interesting to note that the lounge suit has since lost this significance, as it is commonly worn to work or in the evening, as the workplace and transport to it are now cleaner and warmer, whilst a variety of other more casual clothes are often worn at home.

An added complexity of meaning was accorded to the suit in the twentieth century as it was now the attire of Hollywood idols and gained associations of glamour and intense sexuality. It was not until the 1960s and the explosion of youth culture, coupled with an ever-increasing expansion in consumerism, that the suit developed its more contemporary, stuffy and conservative associations. The casual and street culture revolutions reinstated leather and jeans, in the looks of Marlon Brando and James Dean, as the ultimate statements of masculine sex appeal. As a consequence, despite the mods' reconstruction of suited sexuality (oddly returning in the 1990s), the suit soon ended up as something your father wore.

It is perhaps curious, though, that the suit continues to have such strong associations of stoicism, commerce and sheer uniformity when its very history constantly undermines this perspective. The most important empirical factors in this were the various youth movements of the 1960s and 1970s that sought to throw out suits, ties and starched collars together with overthrowing the capitalist ethos of work, thrift and conservatism in favour of jeans, cheesecloth and uncouth hair.

The suit was then reformulated later in the 1970s in flared, tight-fitting and wide-lapelled variants, often in synthetic materials of polyester or velvet, that sought to soften, enliven and, on occasions, seriously sexualize the stoic suit, as in the case of John Travolta in *Saturday Night Fever*. The effect of this was often slightly comical as second-wave feminism had already undermined many more macho and posing stereotypes, such as the hairy-chested medallion man in his skin-tight velvet suit. The 1970s, then, threatened to seriously undermine if not end the reign of the suit in all its forms.

However, the suit returned in the 1980s with a vengeance. A vengeance against all forms of soft-focus effeminacy, pastel colours and politics of caring in asserting a resurgence of shoulder-widening, chest-expanding, city-styled aggression, double-breasted and double-barrelled, and commonly called 'the power look': dressed for success and dressed to kill indeed. The decline of the excesses of the 1980s and the rise of endless deconstructed looks in the 1990s has led some to see the traditional and tailored suit as under threat or even at an end. There is very little evidence to support this hypothesis, as sales of suits since the so-called casual revolution of the 1960s and 1970s have remained comparatively constant, whilst sales of separate trousers and jackets have tended to inversely complement any dip in those of suits (Mintel, 1987). With its persistence on the catwalk, and the increasing use and invention of lighter-weight and easy-to-wear woollen and woollen-mix materials, there is little reason to predict the end of the suit.

Conversely, however, the continuity of the underlying form of the suit still requires consideration. As Anne Hollander in *Sex and Suits* asserts, there is a sense in which the suit has its own history as the mutating uniform of modernity (Hollander, 1994). Hollander writes from a tradition of art history, stressing the consequence of internal design over external controls, and locates the integral significance of form to the evolution of the modern suit and its meanings. What is missing from her analysis is a stronger sense of the wider dynamics, from technology and economics to attitudes and individual lifestyles, that have played their part in shaping the significance of the suit, giving it its strength, resonance and sexiness. Whilst the grace and elegance of the suit may come from the nature and continuity of its design, its eroticism comes more from its emphasis of the male form and, most importantly, from its associations with commerce, success and corporate power: in short from its wearer as well as how and where it is worn.

What is more, the suit still maketh the man most completely. It remains a potent symbol of success, virility and maturity, and the one ensemble from a man's wardrobe that still looks incongruous on a boy – which highlights another, further point. The sexiness of suits comes from their containment and expression, concealment and exposure of the male body, which is why the snap of opening stiff French cuffs around a hirsute and suited wrist has the same sexual charge as unfastening the zip down the back of a little black dress on a beautiful and fully formed woman. Whilst the detail and design of the modern suit endlessly mutates, then, it retains an essential continuity, almost tranquillity of form and meaning amongst the postmodern confusion of contemporary fashion, standing for social tradition and successful, if not necessarily virile, masculinity.

What *is* seemingly changing, however, is the *way* suits are worn. In particular, the casual–formal divide seems to be imploding rapidly, as all or part of suits are worn with or without ties, or put with other more casual clothes as the whole category of smart casual wear expands. This is an important point to make, yet also one which is easily over-emphasized, as Neil Spencer scathingly puts it: 'The suit still rules absolutely what a man must wear to be taken seriously in society' (Spencer, 1992, p. 39). There is indeed little sign of either politicians or office workers, news readers or even weather men throwing off their ties, let alone their suits. The suit has, in one form or another, reigned supreme for over 300 years and is, in short, here to stay. As nothing yet can equal its power, its elegance or its appropriateness on many occasions, this is of little concern. The current return, then, to slimmer, softer and often more quasi-Edwardian styles signifies some dandyism, though not so much an end to the processes set up in the 1980s as much as a melting down; not masculinity in defensive crisis, rather masculinity secure in its own constant narcissistic reinvention.

Conclusion: his story of fashion

> In sum, what is often regarded as the norm of men's clothing – namely, the lack of fashion and the lack of interest by men – is questionable. At most, this has been a recent historical and cultural aberration. (Craik, 1994, p. 197)

In the first instance, the history of fashion is not his story of fashion; it is his or her story of *her* fashion and, most particularly, haute couture. I have also constantly stressed throughout this chapter the complexities and difficulties of understanding the nature and meaning of men's fashion due to the inadequacy of sources and, most importantly, the multiple interpretation of the whole phenomenon. There is some consensus amongst theorists that the contemporary sense of fashion as a primarily female phenomenon is the outcome of wider developments in industrialism and capitalism or, most widely, the formation of modernity (Craik, 1994; Finkelstein, 1991; Hollander, 1994; Wilson, 1985). The recent return to some dandyism in menswear may, then, represent a return to an almost 'pre-modern', or perhaps 'postmodern', sense of men's dress. Nevertheless, for a more theoretical explanation of the development of men's fashion we need to move away from costume history to consider some, more classical, economic and psychological accounts of fashion and modernity, and this is the focus of the second chapter.

Notes

1. A critical perspective is defined here in literary terms where the text or work of art in question is taken and considered in strict isolation from its design, production or interpretation.

2. For examples of the former perspective see: Byrde, 1979; Glynn, 1978; Laver, 1982; Yarwood, 1992; for examples of the latter perspective see: Batterberry and Batterberry, 1982; Hollander, 1988; Roach and Eicher, 1965.

3. The words 'puritan' and 'playboy' and their associated tensions are derived partly from Hoch, 1979.

4. See the work of James Laver and Hardy Amies particularly (Amies, 1994; Laver, 1968, 1982).

5. For an amusing and alarming demonstrative account of the lengths to which the etiquette of suits and ties can go, see image consultant Mary Spillane's *Presenting Yourself: A Personal Image Guide for Men*, 1993.

2

The Classical Tradition

Fashion is often seen as a slightly silly and certainly superficial interest or practice that people associate with youth and dizzy individuals, rather than art, design or society, and consequently tend to dismiss as of only minor importance. The slippery relationship of the high-flown world of specialist haute couture to the more mundane and widespread use of the high street, in particular, has created more coals for the funeral fires of fashion. These factors in turn start to have consequences for the politics of fashion which I consider in Chapter Seven, where I also analyse more contemporary and often more politically motivated perspectives on the development of fashion, such as those derived from feminist, gay or subcultural studies. It is my intention here, therefore, to consider those perspectives which either preceded or laid their roots prior to these later developments. In the first instance, though, it is worth explaining and unpacking the foundations of the study of fashion that were first developed a hundred years or so ago and are still in place today.

The study of fashion, like fashion itself, has its foundations in art and design, or at least in the history of art and design. Indeed, the study of fashion today is still primarily located in the confines of arts departments rather than the social sciences. It is this factor which accounts for much of the apparent and immediate distortion in the study of fashion, or the modern, western and haute couture focus that simultaneously locates and yet often omits consideration of the social context of dress. More importantly, as mentioned in Chapter One, the earliest analyses of fashion were essentially costume histories, graphic accounts of dress through the centuries that were often painstakingly researched and skilfully compiled, yet which opened up a complete omission, in fact a void, of theory.[1] These texts, which are still in production today and used frequently on art and design courses, act as excellent reference texts yet are at their weakest, with some exceptions, in explaining how and why fashion has come to claim its contemporary importance, its politics, or simply its fascination (Chenoune, 1993; Gibbings, 1990; Martin and Koda, 1989). This situation started to change in the 1970s and 1980s with the advent of cultural studies and second wave feminism.[2] The influence of these movements is discussed primarily in Chapter Seven. However, it is worthwhile considering their early forerunners in the study of fashion for, as we shall see, these still form many of the mainstays of the contemporary analyses of fashion: in short, they constitute a classical tradition.

From here to (post) modernity: perspectives on the development of fashion

Over the past hundred years, several perspectives have developed to explain the apparently increasing importance of fashion in western society. These perspectives are grouped relatively easily according to the emphasis they place upon economics, psychology or, more loosely, modernity. In addition, at the end of this section, I include a wider discussion of more contemporary developments and postmodernity in relation to the study of fashion.

Certain points are interesting to note prior to developing a discussion of these perspectives individually. Firstly, all of these perspectives focus almost entirely upon western society and see fashion as an essentially western phenomenon of developed societies. They tend to exclude consideration of eastern dress or fashion design and use in the developing world, which is a serious neglect as western designers regularly plunder the rest of the world for ideas and exploit textiles and skills developed and practised there already. In addition, the contemporary western world of fashion depends increasingly upon the developing world for cheap materials and easily exploited workforces (Phizacklea, 1990).

Secondly, all of the perspectives see fashion as a modern phenomenon, that is, centrally tied up with the development of industrial or consumer capitalism and mercantile trade. This is a point I started to dispute in the previous chapter due to the prevalence of complex designs in dress prior to capitalist development and the universality of styling in dress according to social values, tastes and systems across time and space.

Thirdly, with the exception of some aspects of the psychological perspective, all of these perspectives place a heavy emphasis upon fashion as haute couture. The clear difficulty here is the sense of distance from wider society, and indeed the high street, that this often invokes, creating a notion of fashion as 'up there', 'out there' and 'somewhere' more or less separate from reality and society.

The economic perspective (fashion as consumption)

> Within capitalism, therefore, it becomes possible for both fashion and clothing to be used to construct, signal and reproduce the desire for social mobility between classes as well as class identity itself. (Barnard, 1996, p. 105)

The economic perspective on the development of fashion states primarily that it is the advancement of consumer capitalism which motors the creation, perpetuation and expansion of the fashion industry. Fashion is indeed seen centrally as an *industry* totally reliant on mass production to succeed and, in addition, a primary indicator of the development of surplus production or excess in western advanced society.

Thorstein Veblen in *The Theory of the Leisure Class* (1925) has been the most influential exponent of this position. In particular, he coined the concept of 'conspicuous consumption' that has since passed into common parlance. He posits the idea that as capitalism expands and develops so does a middle or leisure class that seeks to maintain its status through a conspicuous display of its affluence. The focus of his work is primarily upon North American society at the turn of the twentieth century and, as a consequence of this, 'it is especially the rule of the conspicuous waste of goods that finds expression in dress' (Veblen, 1925, p. 167). In other words, dress, and especially haute couture or fashion, is seen as the epitome of superficiality and unnecessary luxury, of primary significance to the new middle classes of North America.

There is a certain common-sense truth in this which may account for the popularity of the work. We quite clearly do not dress according to function or need alone and, in fact, the consumption of clothes increasingly serves no other purpose than to fulfil or express psychological or social, rather than practical, needs. The difficulty is that whilst it is true that we have widely exceeded the practical utility of dress alone, utility still remains and motivates many of the less fashion-conscious groups and individuals that make up society, let alone those who cannot afford to dress for fashion. This raises two further points: firstly, that Veblen's analysis is overly dependent upon attention to a single class or group; and secondly, that individual variation is effectively wiped out in what is an essentially structural perspective.

A second, and interlinked, element to the perspective is the notion that dress acts as a particularly visual display of an individual or group's status. He asserts: 'expenditure on dress has this advantage over other methods, that our apparel is always in evidence and affords an indication of our pecuniary standing to all observers at first glance' (Veblen, 1925, p. 167). As pointed out in the previous chapter, there is some evidence to support the notion that dress acts as a code or performs a signifying function, particularly prior to the twentieth century and in many non-western societies. The difficulty is that as society and dress increase in their complexity of components and populations, the interpretation of dress is ever more uncertain and, in particular, is increasingly contextually dependent. A suit at the opera is an appropriate example of middle-class consumption or attire; a suit at the sea-front often simply looks silly or misplaced.

A more complex aspect of the analysis is the idea that, with the advance of industrial capitalism, men's dress develops along increasingly utilitarian lines: so much so that women's dress alone represents conspicuous consumption, whilst men's dress is indicative of the production that affords the consumption. Or, to put it more simply, men use their wives rather than themselves for the conspicuous display of their affluence. Evidence of this hypothesis centres on the intentionally impractical design of middle-class women's clothing in hampering movement and making many tasks difficult, particularly servile ones. The irony of this is that most servant costumes used to mimic their middle-class counterparts in design and were therefore not particularly practical, with their trailing skirts and confining corsets, conceding only coarseness of cloth and lack of decoration – as much to cheapness as practicality. As pointed out previously, it is also a mistake to see men's dress, even at the height of the Victorian era, as merely a utilitarian uniform, as variations in men's dress and its associated meanings were more complex.

Simmel has provided one of the most simple and enduring economic analyses, otherwise known as the 'trickle-down' theory, of the fashion industry (Simmel, 1973). He states that in capitalist society, where class is of paramount importance in defining identity and personal position, two processes operate simultaneously to maintain the fashion industry: firstly, 'imitation' in that the working or lower classes will seek to imitate the styles of the middle or upper classes as part of an essentially aspirational series of motivations; whilst secondly, the middle or upper classes will seek to separate themselves from the working or lower classes through the process of 'differentiation'. This then sets up a self-perpetuating cycle of imitation and differentiation that partly explains the constant reproduction and reinvention of, in particular, haute couture fashion. Interestingly, McCracken has provided a more contemporary application of the trickle-down theory which also adds gender to the analysis (McCracken, 1985). In examining the contemporary tendency of women's dress to imitate men's, particularly in the use of suited styles in the workplace, he asserts that men have sought to differentiate themselves from women and maintain gender dominance through a 'heroic look' where the suit was reinvested with an intensely masculine sexual charge through the use of wide shoulders, 'V' cuts and pinstripes in the 1980s (see Chapter One). He also argues:

> This understanding allows us to predict not only that men will seek a new style of clothing but also that they will seek a style in which power and authority are re-established. As a superordinate group, men will seek to accomplish an act of differentiation that will do more than recreate an exclusive male clothing style. They will also seek to recreate an exclusive look of authority. (McCracken, 1985, p. 48)

This taps into some of the second-wave feminist points arising around the theme of the New Man considered in more detail in Chapter Three, though it also opens up a further question concerning class.

Whilst, in a sense, aspirational dressing for success is a key motivation in many working-class groups' consumption of fashion, this hardly explains either the equally striking counter-cultural impulses in fashion consumption or the trickle up of many street styles into haute couture (McCracken, 1988). The 'trickle-up' theory, in particular, has developed some credence recently as the likes of Zandra Rhodes and Vivienne Westwood have put punk on the catwalk, whilst Katharine Hamnett made ripped jeans a designer accessory, and Paul Smith is currently reinventing the mod revival. However, it is worth noting the heavy UK emphasis here derived from strong traditions in street style (Polhemus, 1994). Wilson also highlights the technological determinism often implicit in such analyses, as the invention of the Singer sewing machine in 1851, for example, is often seen to herald a design revolution and mass production which, in fact, did not really happen for at least another fifty years, and design itself is perhaps semi-autonomous of technological invention, at least in terms of the intricacies of colour and detail (Wilson, 1985).

More importantly, it is also interesting to note that orthodox Marxism, perhaps the most pervasive of all economic perspectives, has had little to say on consumption, let alone fashion. The Frankfurt School, in the work of Theodor Adorno and Max Horkheimer particularly, has provided one of the most damning indictments of the entire 'culture industry', seen as the new opiate of the masses, as 'it perpetually cheats its consumers of what it perpetually promises' in inducing 'obedience to the social hierarchy' (Adorno and Horkheimer, 1993, p. 38). The 'culture industry' is undifferentiated and ill-defined, to include the entire world of culture from film and TV to art and design, and so renders the individual a mere automaton, if not victim, of society. This has led, not surprisingly, to a re-evaluation within neo-Marxist theory of the role of the consumer, which I wish to consider at the end of this section.

The economic perspective on the development of fashion, then, is often overly simplistic, determinist and one-dimensional in its analysis of more complex phenomena, particularly in terms of meaning and more individual significance – which takes us on to the second perspective.

The psychological perspective (fashion as communication)

The psychological perspective on the development of fashion starts with an acceptance of the premise that dress is not merely a matter of utility or practicality. It is, more importantly, seen as a psychological code or device for displaying individual identity or personality. There is, in similarity to economic theory, some common sense to this as there is little explanation, other than individual idiosyncrasy and personality, as to why we like or dislike certain styles, colours or designs and choose to don one costume rather than another when there are several appropriate to the occasion. In addition, though, the psychological perspective often involves a form of functionalism exemplified in the forerunning work of Charles Flügel who, in *The Psychology of Clothes* (1930), developed an analysis of three of the most primary functions of fashion or dress: firstly, personal protection from climatic conditions; secondly, modesty or concealment in covering up naked skin and particularly the sexual organs; and thirdly, display or signification of status or rank through the use of dress or adornment with often direct or clear social significance.

Later theorists have since criticized the simplicity of Flügel's analysis and also the implicit ethnocentrism and sexism in his interpretations (Barnard, 1996; Barnes and Eicher, 1992; Eicher, 1995). The internal contradictions of such functionalism were exposed through the work of another classical theorist of fashion, James Laver, who rather turned the modesty or concealment function on its head in the notion of the Seduction Principle, where the display of parts of the human form through clothing, or the lack of clothing, was seen to play a part in sexual attraction (Laver, 1969). The Hierarchical Principle, which parallels that of the status and rank function, he connected to men's dress; whilst the fact that his analysis of seductiveness was confined to women's dress left his work wide open to feminist criticism of its sexism (Wilson, 1985). As we shall see in Chapter Three, the principle of seduction through clothing, at least in contemporary western culture, may apply equally well to men's dress.

Given the clear limitations of such perspectives, however, it is perhaps surprising that so much mileage is still made out of psychological theories of fashion. The reason for this lies in the secondary invocation, and constant reinvention, of psychoanalysis. Thus, a more controversial question concerns the notion of the unconscious intervention in dress, a thesis invoked in Alison Lurie's study of *The Language of Clothes* (1981). She starts:

> Long before I am near enough to talk to you on the street, in a meeting, or at a party, you announce your sex, age and class to me through what you are wearing – and very possibly give me important information (or misinformation) as to your occupation, origin, personality, opinions, tastes, sexual desires and current mood. (Lurie, 1981, p. 3)

This statement then sets up the framework for the whole of the analysis that follows, an assumption that 'the clothes maketh the person' and mean something, if not everything, that constitutes them. There is some evidence for the notion that we dress to suit and display ourselves and our personalities, and yet there is also a constant sense of slithering into essentialism that undermines the argument; the idea that a piece of clothing or adornment must necessarily and intrinsically *mean* something or, more insidiously, *reveal* something of our *true* selves. This sense of lurking unconscious drives that we cannot necessarily know ourselves, or even control, yet which give off signals to outsiders, is never very far away in Lurie's detailed discussion of how fashion reflects youth, age, time, space, opinion, personality and sexuality. She even analyses, using physiological evidence, the significance and effects of colour.

It is a seductive analysis, as she writes fluently and displays acute perception. For example, she highlights how the sack shape of the suit covers up a multitude of sins for men, and how many of the more casual styles of contemporary culture rely on physical perfection, with effects that undermine masculinity itself:

> The unathletic white-collar male who affects such styles, however, is taking a risk: presently, he may find himself looking remarkably feeble and podgy in his tight designer jeans and sport shirt while he (and if he is really unlucky, his girl-friend) wait for some trim, well-built auto-mechanic to diagnose his engine trouble. (Lurie, 1981, p. 142)

Lurie's ability to bulldoze the pretence of fashion and expose the strong sense of unease that underlies it is unquestionable, but it remains a problematic analysis on two primary counts. In the first instance, the emphasis on essentialist notions of dress, whilst not intrinsically disastrous, does lead to an undermining of the contradiction, play and complicity that make up the interpretation of dress; and secondly, the stress on individual personality exposes a seriously asocial level to her analysis that underestimates the importance of wider economic or political implications. Her approach to punk, whilst novel, is a primary example: 'At the same time, other aspects of the Punk Look appealed not only for attention, but for the love and care that we give to very small children, especially injured ones' (Lurie, 1981, p. 163). Safety pins and tufts of hair are a particular target here, whilst the far wider aspects of punk, if contentious, are left out completely.

Wilson (1985) has called this intense attention to personality a kind of 'psycho-functionalism' as it ultimately states that clothes perform functions of fulfilling psychological and intrinsic needs. It is also an analysis, though, which, when turned around, leads on to an advanced semiotics of dress where 'we can lie in the language of dress, or try to tell the truth; but unless we are naked and bald it is impossible to be silent' (Lurie, 1981, p. 261).

This analysis of the semiotics of dress and appearance is also what inspires Roland Barthes's most famous analysis of *The Fashion System* (1985). The fashion system is not, as one might assume, an economic system, rather 'fashion is entirely a system of signs' (Barthes, 1985, p. 244). Barthes path-breakingly contrasts 'written clothing', or fashion as linguistic text, with the convention of 'image clothing', or fashion as visual representation, neither of which is 'real' clothing in the sense of the clothes we actually wear. Within this, there is then a series of 'shifters' or linguistic devices that cause a transfer of meaning from one fashion system to another. This is an important set of insights that is difficult to over-estimate in terms of its significance for the analysis of fashion as it essentially sets up the parameters for the whole of the cultural study of fashion and dress that has developed ever since. It also tends to define its limits and pitfalls, as what ensues is an intense and serious analysis of the semiotics of fashion so complex it is hard to decipher and so conceptually advanced it removes fashion almost entirely from its more economic or political, if not sociolinguistic, context. As a consequence, *The Fashion System* ultimately constitutes a study of semiotic methodology rather than an analysis of the full complexity of the production and consumption of fashion.

Joanne Finkelstein in *The Fashioned Self* has produced perhaps the most convincing psychologically driven analysis of fashion (Finkelstein, 1991). Her central concern is with the conflation of reality and appearance through fashion leading on to the perpetuation of the myth that appearances 'mean something' and are constitutive of character or personality. She focuses on the increasing concern with physique, fashion and appearance in the twentieth century, and says that:

> This suggests that the perpetual conspiracy which allows the artificial complexion and body shape to be seen as a natural representation of character, and the fashioned styles of beauty to be accepted as expression of human sensibility, remains as convincing as ever. (Finkelstein, 1991, p. 3)

In so doing, she criticizes Hollander's implicit solipsism and essentialism and runs contrary to Lurie's analysis of visual linguistics in asserting forcefully that 'the self has become a mass-produced, market product; buy this in order to be that' (Finkelstein, 1991, p. 172).[3] Finkelstein's work is uneasily and, on occasions, contradictorily located into a social and psychological framework that incorporates Eliasian elements, as the formation of modern men's tailoring, in particular, is seen as an example of the 'civilizing process'.[4] Whilst such analysis produces insights into the gendered use of dress and shape (for example in the case of shoulder pads, which in the 1940s were used to heighten a man's stature and yet emphasize a woman's waistline, therefore differentiating genders with the same product), there is, in common with similar semi-functionalist accounts of fashion, a tendency towards simplicity in analysis of the production and consumption of fashion.

Malcolm Barnard attempts to re-evaluate the psycho-linguistic aspects of dress in *Fashion as Communication* (1996). In particular, he adopts Derrida's notion of undecidability in showing how dress constantly creates and destroys meaning, making it simultaneously meaningful and meaningless and infinitely dynamic. A clear difficulty he recognizes here, though, is the slippage from dress as function, to fashion as contested meaning and interpretation, although he disputes the ease of the distinction. As a result, the psychological perspective overall tends to address the importance of dress rather than the question of fashion which, incidentally, is in stark contrast to the perspective of modernity, as we shall see.

The modern perspective (fashion as contradiction)

Fashion is modernist irony. (Wilson, 1985, p. 15)

The perspective of modernity on the development of fashion seeks to undermine the determinism implicit equally in economic and psychological perspectives via the more open concept of modernity. There is an immediate difficulty in defining the term, which exponents of the theory, let alone theorists of postmodernity, are apt to point out. At its most concrete, the concept opens up to scrutiny and relevance a whole series of social and political, as well as economic, developments that characterize the twentieth century. These include: consumerism, individualism, and the development of lifestyles around sport and leisure, as well as mass production, the media and the city, as central in creating openings for the fashion industry. As a result, it is argued that 'the word "modernity" attempts to capture the essence of both the cultural and subjective experience of capitalist society and all its contradictions' (Wilson, 1985, p. 63).

In addition, it is pointed out more concretely that many of the stylistic developments in fashion have accompanied similar developments in the world of art itself in making shape, colour and design into new constructions. In this sense, the society-level notion of moder*nity* is very much interconnected with the stylistic development of moder*nism*. Anne Hollander in *Seeing Through Clothes*, for example, argues that fashion has followed traditions in figurative art in terms of form and design; whilst Wilson makes similar claims in *Adorned in Dreams* that modern fashion has echoed the forms of modern art (Hollander, 1988; Wilson, 1985).

The primary importance of the concept of modernity, though, is its capacity to capture the contradictory and dynamic nature of the fashion phenomenon: the restless and dissatisfied desire for something new that permeates and underpins modern industrial capitalism. Thus, in one sense, the concept of modernity is far more accurate as a *description* of the practice of fashion and yet this is precisely its weakness, its lack of more *explanatory* power. The concept of modernity expresses much, yet explains very little. On top of this, the concept of postmodernity has rapidly overtaken that of modernity as a descriptive, and perhaps also more explanatory, tool in analysing the system of fashion, a question to which I now turn.

Contemporary developments: postmodernity

More recently, the concept of postmodernity has tended to take over from modernity as a means of explaining and understanding developments in contemporary western society. There is no one theory of postmodernity and it is not my intention to provide a definitive account of its importance. Nonetheless, there is a sense in which the concept and theories applied to it have increased in their significance for the study of fashion and society more widely. The immediate difficulty lies in the definition of the term and it is first of all necessary to separate the notion of postmodern*ism*, as a series of artistic and stylistic developments in the arts, literature and architecture, from postmodern*ity*, or the more social, economic and sometimes political term used to understand and/or explain developments in society during the twentieth century and particularly since the Second World War.

However, additional difficulties are encountered in relation to the question of whether the theory of postmodernity is necessarily also tied up with either postindustrial theory, primarily an economic perspective emphasizing the importance of multinational corporatism and the separation of ownership and control, or poststructural theory, which seeks to implode the division of action and structure often through the concept and practice of discourse. It is my concern here, therefore, to consider the theory of postmodernity primarily in relation to the study of fashion and not in relation to wider questions of social theory.

There is, as yet, no single full-length study of the significance of fashion to postmodernity and, similarly no theory of the importance of postmodernity to the study of fashion. However, numerous contemporary theorists have used fashion as an example to highlight specific aspects of their theories, and it is easy to extrapolate the importance of central concepts to the study of fashion. The primary application of postmodernity theory to the study of fashion comes through its analysis of the concept and practice of consumer society. Postmodernity theory primarily assumes that consumerism, as concept and practice, acquires increased significance under conditions of what is called sometimes late or high capitalism.[5] It is asserted that, in particular, people spend increasing degrees of time consuming as opposed to producing, and that these activities therefore come to gain added significance in the formation of their individual and group identities. As dress constitutes a significant and visual factor in the formation of individual and group identities, there is a clear conflation of fashion and consumption that is potentially self-perpetuating in its importance. This accounts partly for the primacy of fashion as an example of the excesses of consumer society under conditions of postmodernity. At a more common-sense level, the high cost, high turnover world of haute couture also illustrates the nature of postmodernity itself, in its heightening of the importance of representation and appearance to the construction of personal identity (see, for example, Faurschou, 1988).

There are similarly applications of the concepts of commodification and signification to the study of fashion. Commodification refers to the increasing involvement of goods, services and indeed everyday life in processes of advertising, promotion and monetary exchange. The privatization of health, education and transportation form primary examples of this process, as do many leisure activities and the explosion of financial services for every real, and imagined, need and anxiety. Signification refers to the process of increasing significance of social, symbolic and representational value applied to commodities and indeed all aspects of everyday life. Primary examples of this process include the logos and design cultures of the 1980s, advertising, and the sometimes ludicrous status values attached to goods such as Levi's 'original' 501 jeans, 'it's a Sony' stereos, or BMW's 'ultimate driving machine'.

Similarly, for Jean Baudrillard, dress and fashion form primary examples of the 'commodity sign', as an axiom of where the processes of commodification and signification come together (Baudrillard, 1981, 1983). The secondary argument that the sign value is increasingly autonomous of the commodity value is also highlighted in the ludicrous costs of haute couture, as is the desire for authenticity in the construction of 'classics' and individual designer styles differentiated from their imitators. More importantly, this also ties up with wider societal processes of 'reproduction', 'simulation', and their implied impacts of uncertainty and confusion of social values, in short 'the death of the social', as the significance of fashion and dress is seen as increasingly out of control and anarchic. The processes of reproduction and simulation refer, in particular, to the importance of the media and similar visual cultures in reproducing goods so effectively that the simulation, or visual representation on TV, give greater significance or status than the actual goods or services. Moreover, this is then seen to lead to increasing confusion and uncertainty concerning what is real or authentic, in turn rocking the foundations of tradition and social values; a vision which, in its most extreme form, is almost apocalyptic.

For Fredric Jameson, there are similarly applications of postmodernity theory to the study of fashion in terms of the concept of 'depthless culture', for the fascination of fashion is often the fascination of surfaces, of reflections, of packaging, and of seduction (Jameson, 1984). In addition, for some feminists these processes have had more positive consequences and led to the disruption of gendered traditions in fashion as 'the dichotomy whereby fashion is identified with women and oppositional style with masculine subcultures was erased in postmodern fashion' (Evans and Thornton, 1989, p. 74). These are, however, questions to which I wish to give additional consideration in Chapter Seven.

A rather more 'grounded' perspective, perhaps, is provided by Bourdieu in his study of *Distinction: A Social Critique of the Judgement of Taste* (1984). Bourdieu's detailed observation of the habits and lifestyles of the French, paying particular attention to factors such as dress, haircuts and dining out, provides an excellent example of the more social importance of fashion in forming and maintaining personal or group status or identity as 'taste classifies, and it classifies the classifier' (Bourdieu, 1984, p. 6). The difficulty is that this often leads to a reinvention of models of class and stratification rather than a more radical analysis of the complexities of culture, gender and identity. Interestingly, his conceptualization of the paperchase of social position echoes Simmel's earlier analysis of imitation and differentiation cited previously, although he stresses differently the importance of 'cultural intermediaries' in sustaining the process.[6] His analysis of fashion tends to illustrate these points:

> Fashion is the latest fashion, the latest difference. An emblem of class (in all senses) withers once it loses its distinctive power. When the miniskirt reaches the mining village of northern France, it's time to start again. (Bourdieu, 1993, p. 135)

The ultimate application of postmodernity theory to the study of fashion comes in the work of the Krokers, whose 'hysteria' concerning everything from Eurythmics videos to Calvin Klein advertising teeters on self-parody:

> Indeed, if fashion cycles now appear to oscillate with greater and greater speed, frenzy and intensity of circulation of all the signs, that is because fashion, in an era when the body is the inscribed surface of events, is like Brownian motion in physics: the greater the velocity and circulation of its surface features, the greater the internal movement towards stasis, immobility, and inertia. (Kroker and Kroker, 1988, p. 45)

The implicit nihilism of this statement brings us neatly back in full postmodern circle to Baudrillard, but the irony of all these studies in postmodernity is that none actually ranks as a serious and detailed consideration of fashion itself – which returns us, once again, to the classical tradition.

Conclusion: the classical tradition

During this chapter, I have attempted to document and unpack the formation of what I have called a 'classical tradition' concerning the study of fashion, that locates the analysis of dress within the context of the arts, haute couture or, most widely, modernity. The theory of postmodernity has done much to disrupt this perspective on fashion and yet provides a very fragmented set of insights into its more contemporary significance.

The concentration on men's dress or menswear in all of the aforementioned analyses of fashion is decidedly thin. In particular, the economic perspective, whilst paying some attention to matters of gender, makes a series of serious assumptions concerning gender identity – most particularly that women are decorative and men are not – which are easily criticized and produce an essentially sexist *his*tory of *her* fashion (see also Chapter One). The psychological perspective appears at first more fruitful, as issues of sexual identity are readily included in the psychology of fashion; yet what is not on the whole included is a consideration of the connection of gendered psychology to the wider economic or political (if not social) context, or even a sense in which gender identity is more than a matter of individual personality.[7] The perspective of modernity is simultaneously the most all-encompassing and yet the least explanatory, and perhaps represents an untapped potential for making connections across masculinity and gender identity, to the terrain of (post)modern society. Meanwhile, all these analyses tend to neglect the significance of dress or fashion for the *wearer* as opposed to the onlooker (Corrigan, 1993; Davis, 1992). This leads to an additional difficulty of resolving the significance of fashion for the individual with its wider social, economic or political importance. This issue is as yet unaddressed, partly as a result of the lack of empirical or ethnographic – as opposed to theoretical or interpretive – study of dress and fashion.[8]

Apart from the critique one can apply to any of the perspectives individually, they have several factors in common which help to explain the conspicuous lack of attention to men's dress. Firstly, the study of fashion, as I have already mentioned, has tended to develop within the confines of art and design and, in addition, this has then led to an emphasis upon haute couture. Haute couture, until quite recently, was primarily the preserve of fashion design for women only, in turn centred on the notion that the art form is essentially the female form and, furthermore, the problematic idea that the female body rather than the male body remains the primary symbol of aesthetic beauty.[9]

Secondly, fashion, for the past century at least, was widely seen as a feminine phenomenon. One explanation of this is simply economic, as middle-class women, in particular, were confined to the private sphere of consumption, shopping and personal pleasure, a role also reconstructed since the Second World War (see Chapter Six). Therefore, put simply, women rather than men *were* the market for fashion. Thirdly, though, this does not explain *why* women were put in this position or *why* men were apparently merely producers and not consumers of fashion.[10] This question would seem to centre on modern, western and gendered attitudes that men are not interested in fashion, other than on 'their' women, or that they are 'outside' fashion: in short, fashion is not seen as 'masculine'. In Chapter Three, though, I wish to consider how the male form and men's fashion, particularly in the 1980s, were reconstructed quite intentionally to include, incorporate, and even emphasize masculinity and men.

Notes

1. See Batterberry, 1982; Byrde, 1979; Flügel, 1965; Glynn 1978; Laver, 1982; Roach, 1965; Yarwood, 1992; for varying examples of art- or design-oriented costume histories of fashion.

2. See in particular Hebdige, 1979; McRobbie, 1984; and Wilson, 1985 as important examples of this process of analysis, as well as Wolf's inflamed polemic *The Beauty Myth*, 1991.

3. Finkelstein (1991) in particular criticizes Hollander's historical analysis of dress as autonomous from its social context in design and form (see Hollander, 1988, and Chapter One).

4. Elias was a highly influential sociologist whose major work *The Civilizing Process* was an attempt to document the formation of modern society from medievalism to industrialism (see Elias, 1978, 1982).

5. The concept of late capitalism was primarily used in the work of Fredric Jameson, whilst that of high capitalism underpins the work of Anthony Giddens. In each case there

is a clear emphasis placed upon such factors as consumption, multinational corporatism and the separation of ownership and control to characterize the latter part of the twentieth century (Giddens, 1990; Jameson, 1984).

6. Cultural intermediaries are the media informers of society: magazine writers and editors, TV hosts and personal consultants who advise the middle classes on the detailed etiquette of their status.

7. There are perhaps one or two exceptions to this point, primarily in the work of Joanne Finkelstein and in Michael Solomon's more interdisciplinary collection (see Finkelstein, 1991; Solomon, 1985).

8. One of the apparent exceptions to this is anthropological work on dress and fashion, yet Corrigan is equally critical of the rather descriptive level of most of these analyses (see Barnes and Eicher, 1992; Corrigan, 1993; Eicher, 1995).

9. There is, perhaps, some evidence that this is changing, as male muscularity

in contemporary society is currently
escalating in its status and
significance, with accompanying
academic studies of the male form,
and there is strong evidence that this
rise in interest in the muscular male
form is limited to Judeo-Christian

society (see Cooper, 1995; Dutton,
1995; Pfeil, 1994; Scott and Morgan,
1993).
10. This justifies, to a limited extent of
course, the ideas of Veblen discussed
earlier (Veblen, 1925).

3

Private Investigations: Interpretations on the Theme of the New Man

> Child of our time, the new man is all about us – rising like Venus from the waves or Adonis from the shaving foam, strutting his stuff across posters, calendars, magazines and birthday cards, peering nonchalantly down from advertising hoardings, dropping his trousers in the launderette. He is everywhere. (Chapman, 1988, pp. 225–6)

The New Man arose as a primarily media-driven phenomenon in the 1980s. It was said that, as a result of the impact of second-wave feminism in particular, men and masculinity were under attack, and a new form of masculinity that was more caring, nurturing and sensitive – or, alternatively, more narcissistic, passive and introspective – was developing. Furthermore, like the phoenix from the flames, the New Man in the 1980s was emerging from the ashes of vilified Old Man in the 1970s. The advertisement for Calvin Klein's Eternity, showing a man cradling an infant, formed a very good example of this kind of iconography.

Evidence for these claims was distinctly scattered, covering everything from Levi's advertising campaigns to the rise of designer fashion for men; from the cult of Californian muscularity to the benefits of toyboys; and from pornography for women to Athena's 'L'Enfant' poster and postcard nudes.[1] Attention to these developments did not only come from the media. Before long, academic interest, particularly from the already expanding fields of study in masculinity and sexual politics, also increased. Immediate questions were raised concerning whether the New Man existed outside of media hype and what impact second-wave feminism was or was not having on the concept and practice of masculinity in the 1980s – and what this meant for women.[2]

It is my primary intention, then, in this chapter, to explore these questions and their suggested solutions in detail through a discussion of more academic responses to the phenomenon of the New Man. In addition, though, I wish to propose that the New Man was not simply the product of the media, or even of responses to second-wave feminism; he was rather the crystallization of consequences in economics, marketing, political ideology, demography and, most widely, consumer society in the

1980s. In so doing, I am also intentionally setting up many of the parameters of succeeding chapters.

It is the primary purpose of this particular chapter, therefore, to explore the increasing contemporary concern with men's fashion through a discussion of some of the central images associated with it. The first section is a discussion of the significance of images of masculinity in general, and a delineation of those most central to the study of masculinity in the 1980s. There then follows a critical analysis of the various perspectives taken to explain and interpret the rise in interest in men's fashion, the New Man and the images of masculinity attendant with it. The third section draws out some of the potential implications of the processes and developments taking place in relation to men's fashion, masculinity and consumer society. Lastly, a short study is also provided of the advertising campaigns for Levi's 501 jeans.

Images of masculinity

> One would think that writing about images of male sexuality would be as easy as anything. We live in a world saturated with images, drenched in sexuality. But this is one of the reasons why it is in fact difficult to write about. Male sexuality is a bit like air – you breathe it in all the time, but you aren't aware of it much. (Dyer, 1985, p. 28)

Images of masculinity are, I assert, an increasingly pervasive aspect of consumer-oriented society. Consequently, they are everywhere: from the military virility of Rambo to the anguished passivity of Merchant Ivory, from Mel Gibson's and Bruce Willis's lovable roguery to Tom Cruise's and Brad Pitt's toyboy cuteishness, from Hollywood idols like Rock Hudson and Cary Grant to the cinematic crusades of Kevin Costner, from George Michael's designer stubble to Michael Jackson's squeal appeal, from Bruce Springsteen's heterosexual growl to Jimmy Somerville's homosexual falsetto, from J. R. Ewing to Dirty Den, from *Arena* and *GQ* to *For Women* and *My Guy*, from Armani and Gucci to Next and Top Man, from high street postcard nudes to Woolworth's pin-up calendars, from the Chippendales and London Knights to the Clothes Show model and the *Sun* newspaper's 'page seven fellas', from Rodeo Drive to the TV, from Milan to the living room, and from multi-gyms to high street shopping: he comes – the new man of narcissism – glowing, sweating and grinning, an exploding signifier of the so-called 'postmodern condition' (Baudrillard, 1983; Jameson, 1984, 1988; Lyotard, 1984).[3]

It is the very pervasiveness of this signification that makes the task of focusing any concentration on masculinity so difficult. Masculinity is frequently ill-defined as an omnipresent, previously assumed and unacknowledged construct that is, in fact, seen in constant relation to its opposites of femininity, otherness and the stigmatization of women, gay men and black sexuality (Carrigan *et al.*, 1985; Connell, 1987; Craig, 1992; Mercer and Julien, 1988; Staples, 1982). Consequently, to try and anchor this discussion of masculinity and men's fashion, I wish to concentrate attention on the phenomenon of the New Man and, more specifically, I wish to consider men's fashion and images of masculinity as represented in men's style magazines, TV advertising and men's fashion promotions. In addition, I wish to set this discussion in the temporal context of the 1980s, the period in which the phenomenon of the New Man, and all that came with it, not so accidentally exploded.

Images of masculinity are pumped through the media, witnessed on trains, splashed upon posters and endlessly paraded in mail-order and high-street shopping. Yet despite this apparent plethora, the content of these representations remains quite extraordinarily fixed. The men concerned are always young, usually white, particularly muscular, critically strong-jawed, clean shaven (often all over), healthy, sporty, successful, virile, and ultimately sexy (see Plate One). Consequently, whilst other images of masculinity do necessarily exist these are not used to advertise men's fashion and accessories or to sell anything other than their silliness: doddery old men, screaming queens and ghetto-blasting black guys. In a basic sense, what we are talking about here are the social divisions between men's bodies but, in addition to this, another division is enacted (Scott and Morgan, 1993).

I wish to assert that in the period in question two central images of masculinity came to dominate men's fashion as the most valorized and advertised. These two representations were, and are, entirely constructed according to the clothing and accessorizing of the same male form and are therefore two sides of the same coin. I call the heads side of the coin the *corporate power look*, where formal work clothes, and particularly the suit, were used to cover yet accentuate the same masculine, mesomorphic physical shape (see Plate Two). It was a particularly self-conscious acting out of the visual role of the successful city executive consisting of dark, broadly cut, double-breasted suits, striped shirts, Oxford brogues, braces, briefcases and, of course, the fast car, Filofax and personal phone, all completing the look of a man in control and on the up. Aspirationalism and corporate success were, in fact, the key elements (Mort, 1988).

I call the tails side of the coin the *outdoor casual*, as the muscular hunk concerned was usually seen outside stripping off his white T-shirt, easing himself into or out of his jeans, sweating in leather, or doing things with machines. He was also sometimes seen as the working-class or football casual with sufficient affluence for designer clothes (Spencer, 1992). The emphasis was placed on his physicality through the clothes and through the lack of clothes, the intensely phallocentric 'now you see it, now you don't' of his manhood.

This dualistic distinction was occasionally interpreted as a class distinction, but in reality, fashion-conscious working-class *and* middle-class men wore, and still wear, suits *and* jeans. In fact, the sexy suit look was often a working-class look: a sign of young lads on the make. More importantly, the distinction was also interpreted as one of mind and body, of heads and tails, or butts, but the problem here was the sheer physicality of the corporate power look in widening shoulders, expanding chests and connecting larynx to crotch in ties, stripes and the ever-deepening 'V' cut of the suit. The most convincing interpretation of this distinction was one of formality and informality, or work and leisure, or, as Neil Spencer put it: 'More than ever, it seems, male Britain is divided into two breeds: those who wear suits to work and those who don't' (Spencer, 1992, p. 47). There is a slippery slope of collapsing concepts here, though, as suits were, and are, increasingly worn for dressy social purposes, and jeans and T-shirts have their origins as American manual workwear. The power of the white T-shirt and worn jeans look also centres heavily on the associations of physical work involved. Examples of the corporate power look and the outdoor casual in the period in question included American soap opera stars in *Dallas* and *Dynasty*, plus their UK equivalents in *Chancer* and *Capital City*, reinventions of 1950s Hollywood iconography and upmarket men's magazines like *GQ* on the one hand; and of advertising for Levi's jeans and fruit drinks, muscular nudes on posters, plus pornography for women on the other.

The outdoor casual has attracted particular attention not least in relation to advertising for Levi's 501 jeans (see the study at the end of this chapter). Still significantly, though, the second half of the story concerns what I have called the corporate power look. Whilst less focused on one central product (although the suit came perilously close), the meteoric rise of the overall executive *look* was critical. It was critical on several counts: firstly, it reflected a wider phenomenon of yuppiedom; secondly, it also projected a new and highly sexualized image of masculinity into what was previously perceived as a dull area of men's dress; and thirdly, it tapped into and exploited the rise of 'lifestyle' as concept and practice, as it was not only the suit and tie alone that created the look, rather the plethora of accessories from BMWs, boxer shorts and designer label gels to Dockland apartments, storecards and conspicuous belt buckles (Spencer, 1992). More importantly, part of the appeal of this look lay in the increasing emphasis upon fashion itself as a part of lifestyle or as constitutive of particularly aspirational parts of personality, and a return to traditional masculine values of money, work and success (see Plate Three). As Peter York put it:

We all know that suit: double-breasted, padded shoulders, no vents, a bit boxy, with the lapels crossing in big, low-cut, diagonal slashes to show quite a lot of tie. A *Chancer* suit, an estate agent suit, a New City Boy suit. *The* suit of the mid/late eighties. (York, 1995, p. 20)

The perspective taken here contrasts sharply with the work of some other authors in the area, particularly Frank Mort and Sean Nixon, who have stressed strongly the degree of plurality in contemporary representations of men and masculinity (Mort, 1988, 1996; Nixon, 1992, 1993). Much of the evidence for their assertions centres on a reading of images of masculinity presented in men's style magazines and, in particular, Ray Petri's work with *The Face* and other titles which was often perceived, I think correctly, to start to play with the pieces of masculine appearance. Whilst I do not wish to dispute the importance of such developments, their impact temporally and spatially was still often limited to fashion-literate and young, gay male circles. Thus, whilst I acknowledge that other images of masculinity do of necessity exist, these are not hegemonic or dominant in the context of the wider society in the way that what I have called the corporate power look or the outdoor casual clearly were and, what is more, still are.

Two recent factors affecting these representations, though, are the development of New Laddism, considered in more detail in Chapter Five; and the rise of the New Waif, often following similar developments in mainstream or popular representations of women and most importantly the stardom of supermodel Kate Moss, particularly in the form of the pasty-looking icons of Britpop. The most important point to make here is that each of these developments has emerged primarily as a counter-reaction to dominant representations of masculinity as muscular or virile, suited for success or stripped down to torso and jeans, adding further testimony to their dominance in the period in question.

In conclusion to this section, then, it seems clear that, contradictorily, not only have we witnessed an increasing pervasiveness of images of masculinity and an escalating significance of fashion, dress and appearance within this, but we have also seen an equally increasing focusing of these representations into a dependence upon traditional values of virility and success, seriously sexualized in advertising and marketing campaigns. Ironically, then, the New Man expressed many very old views and values.

Interpretations

Images of masculinity are variously and, on occasions, contradictorily interpreted, yet one factor which remains constant is the assertion that these representations *construct* masculinity as part of a dynamic process of interpretation and implication. Masculinity is not seen as a fixed essence reflected in representation; rather the representations create the sense of masculinity as essence (Craig, 1992). Significantly, it is also argued that there is no one masculinity constructed or represented, rather a series of masculinities that are hierarchically ordered according to colour, class and sexual orientation (Connell, 1987, 1995). Images of white, middle-class and heterosexual masculinity are therefore hegemonic whilst those of black, working-class or homosexual masculinity are subordinate. In addition, the hegemonic and subordinate are mutually reinforcing of each other. Therefore, what we are often considering when looking at images or representations of masculinity are not solely the overt images or representations themselves, but the complex and covert conceptions of masculinity upon which they are premised. More importantly still, there is also the complex process of the interpretation of the viewer–viewee relationship, and most perspectives upon representations of masculinity and men's fashion attempt to explore and develop this relationship. There are primarily four sets of studies which have attempted to enter into this discussion, derived from a mixture of cultural and sociological sources, which I shall consider in turn.

The first of these contributions came, not surprisingly, from media studies. Laura Mulvey wrote in a very influential article, 'Visual pleasure and narrative cinema', that the images of women in cinema and TV were constructed as objects to be looked at as part of a patriarchal construction of exhibitionism and voyeurism (Mulvey, 1975). Mulvey argued strongly that gender imagery created and compounded traditional roles of activity and passivity for men and women respectively, where men looked and women were looked at. This assertion was later criticized on several counts: Steve Neale highlighted the importance of the repression of homosexuality in men looking, or rather not looking, at other men (Neale, 1982, 1983); Ian Green sought to open up what happened when men did indeed start to look at other men or identify alternatively with women (Green, 1984); and Gaines, Rodowick and other feminists criticized Mulvey's depiction of female viewers as overly passive and ultimately racist (Gaines, 1986; Kirkham and Thumim, 1993; Rodowick, 1982; Stockbridge, 1990). This racist element was also explored primarily in relation to male homosexuality in the work of Kobena Mercer and Isaac Julien (Mercer and Julien, 1988). As a result, whilst the central tenets of Mulvey's work remained intact, the picture was clouded significantly through the incorporation of racial, sexual, or indeed individual and gendered, variations in looking and representation.

Secondly, women's studies not surprisingly started to turn attention towards the wider implications of the viewer–viewee relationship for women. Most powerfully, Naomi Wolf argued forcefully that the image or appearance of femininity and beauty was both myth and uncompromising reality: the unnatural demands placed upon women to conform to appropriate representations of femininity culminated in high levels of anxiety, depression and eating disorders (Wolf, 1991). This did not of course account for similar impacts upon men in terms of narcissism or pumping iron, often seen as primarily parallel phenomena for men in the 1980s. However, feminism was not silent on these points either. Rowena Chapman, for example, summed up much feminist opinion in asserting that developments in male narcissism and expanding interest in men's fashion represented a hijacking of femininity or a 'have your cake and eat it' situation, where men could don the costumes of femininity – sometimes literally – without living with the consequences. She also asserted that such representations of masculinity remained deeply phallocentric, as the penis was, necessarily, never seen though constantly invoked and empowered through the implication of the phallus (Chapman, 1988). This happened not only through the hyper-masculinization of other parts of the male body or the fetishization of men's fashion but through the use of penis substitutes from guns to saxophones (Fiske, 1987). The emphasis placed on the defensiveness and phallocentrism of many of these representations of men, masculinity and men's fashion in the 1980s led on to the assertion that such images did not so much challenge as reinforce or valorize traditional definitions of masculinity and male power. This was then seen to tie up with the expansion of marketing of men's fashion, often seen partly as a design-driven initiative as more women and gay men began to design collections for men as well as women, and partly as a matter of economics in the creation of new fashion and lifestyle markets for high-earning and high-spending male consumers: yuppie markets for yuppies (Ash, 1989).

The difficulty of this perspective, though, is that it did not fully consider the relationship of viewer to viewee as previously outlined. Even if the viewee was partly an intentional valorization of masculinity, whether through pose, exposure of physicality or fetishism of clothing and accessories, what did this mean for the viewer, who now perceived this as the object and not the subject of valour, particularly if the viewer were male or identified as masculine? As a continuation, then, this raised the central question of the *reconstruction* of masculinity *through* consumption, and particularly in terms of the processes of looking, as Craik asserted:

> Changing conventions of men's fashion have entailed re-worked attributes of masculinity that have transformed male bodies into objects of the gaze, of display and decoration. This radically undercuts the Victorian and post-Victorian idea of masculinity as the display of restraint in a disciplined body. (Craik, 1994, p. 203)

Some writers have also started to raise additional issues concerning the increasing significance of men looking at other men in specific locations such as the City or Soho in London, often incorporating newly invented and ill-defined notions and concepts from other disciplines such as homosociality and social space, derived from literary theory and geography respectively (Mort, 1996).[4] In conclusion, then, there is quite clearly a tension or contradiction of content and meaning, as images of masculinity, whilst not necessarily challenging patriarchal ideology, are still not entirely what they seem.

Thirdly, then, this notion of reconstruction of masculinity through the practices of representation and consumption also underpins men's studies of masculinity, which have tended to assert that these images *do* imply an important development in conceptions of masculinity which is also potentially applied in practice (Craig, 1992; Dyer, 1989; Kirkham and Thumim, 1993; Mort, 1986, 1988; Pumphrey, 1989). They claim that the increasing pervasiveness of images of masculinity, particularly when tied to definitions of sexuality, tends to rupture the traditional mode of masculine activity and feminine passivity (the idea that men look and women are looked at) and, indeed, the increasing role of men as consumers, as opposed to producers, of fashions and representations of themselves is seen as increasingly central. The argument here centres upon the notion that masculinity and masculine identity were traditionally defined through work, or production, rather than through consumption, which was seen more as a feminine preserve, as in the stereotype of the happy housewife going shopping, typical of advertising for washing powder. These are points I otherwise wish to unpack in Chapter Six. However, I do at this point wish to raise the question of whether masculinity was ever solely defined through production and, in addition, whether the work role excludes the role of consumption, particularly in relation to fashion: dress for the office has often required significant attention to, and indeed consumption of prevailing styles and fashions for men as well as women.

Ultimately, though, this implies a certain feminizing or undermining of traditional masculinity in concept and potentially in practice. There is, though, no simple relationship or impact of representation upon practice, due to varying personal interpretation and the complex relationship of personal perception to personal practice (Seiter, 1989). People do not necessarily practice what they aspire to or preach. More importantly, an immediate issue is raised as to the representations of masculinity themselves. Many writers point out that these are often self-contradictory. The passivity of the posing male is counterposed with the implied activity and control of his muscularity, smart suit or sexy clothes. Models are often seen to stare up, away or through the viewer, or are situated in relation to often very passive women, or as part of a group of men imparting greater power and therefore deflecting the viewer's activity of looking at them, on several levels (Craig, 1992; Dyer, 1989, 1992, 1993; Mort, 1988). In conclusion, then:

> On the one hand, this is a visual medium, these men are there to be looked at by women. On the other hand, this does violence to the codes of who looks and who is looked at (and how), and some attempt is instinctively made to counteract this violation. (Dyer, 1989, p. 199)

Fourthly, in gay studies, writers have asserted that gay male culture, in terms of its exploration of male sexuality and its representations, is exploited by these mainstream images which essentially fetishize gay sexuality and: 'Gay men have to continually contest their subordination and resist definitions of themselves that are often rooted in heterosexual men's fetishism' (Rutherford, 1988, p. 59). The 1980s image of the outdoor casual with muscular torso and figure-hugging 501s is indeed an image derived directly from the processes of gay sexualization in the 1970s and, in addition, much advertising of fashion and accessories exploits patterns of gay male production and consumption, in content and style, without acknowledgement.[5] This point is premised partly upon the assumption that gay men form an important consumption group due to high levels of spending power, particularly on fashion products, a point with which I take issue in Chapter Seven. Nevertheless, the lack of any overt recognition of a specifically gay consumer group remains significant. Men's style magazines (with the exception of the queer-driven *Attitude* or *Genre*) are a primary example of this process, splashing glossy and homoerotic imagery upon pages of advertising for fashion goods and accessories, and therefore appealing directly to a gay readership, whilst still defensively asserting the heterosexuality of their readers in articles on sex and women (see Chapter Five). More importantly, positive representations of alternative male sexuality, it is asserted, are essentially 'symbolically annihilated' through exclusion, misrepresentation or marginalization of gay men (Fejes, 1992; Gross, 1989; Hanke, 1992; Russo, 1987).

Consequently, there is little to query concerning the oppression of positive representations of gay sexuality; the query concerns the impact and implications of the implicit homosexuality in selling representations of masculinity and men to other men. Some writers, most recently Mark Simpson, are more positive on this point, asserting: 'Traditional heterosexuality cannot survive this reversal, particularly because it brings masculinity into perilously close contact with that which must always be disavowed: homosexuality' (Simpson, 1994, p. 4).[6] The difficulty here is the question of interpretation and intention, as it is entirely uncertain that any such representation is intentionally homoerotic or is interpreted sexually by heterosexuals.

Whilst sexualized advertising and rising interest in men's fashion may signify some disruption of conceptions of traditional masculinity, it remains an open question as to whether this then implies any significant impact upon practice or attitudes, that is, apart from spending, and this is the key question raised in the following section.[7]

Implicating and impacting masculinities

Designer clothes are not the concern solely of the southern yuppy classes. They reflect a masculinity that has partly detached itself from its formative links to traditional class identities. It has become aspirational and more narcissistic, affected by the consumer market and the purchasing of style and appearance. (Rutherford, 1988, p. 39)

Most attention to men's fashion and images of masculinity tends to concentrate, as already highlighted, on interpretations of representations and excludes consideration of causes or effects, implications or impacts upon men themselves or within society as a whole. Therefore I first of all wish to contextualize the development of the aforementioned rise in interest in men's fashion, and the simultaneous increasing concentration on images of masculinity, within the social, economic and political context of the 1980s, and to argue that it is no accident and no coincidence that these developments took place at the same time.

Firstly, economically, Conservative and Reaganite governments sought to deregulate the economy and open up more areas of society to the free market. This most notoriously included such areas as health, housing and education, yet also had a profound impact upon employment. Manufacturing industries, as is well known, were in steady decline since the Second World War, if not earlier, and this formed a major factor in increasing unemployment. Service industries were expanding over the same period, yet were still operating under a series of financial controls. When these controls were lifted there was a resulting expansion in employment in the service and financial sectors including banking and insurance, the City and stockbroking, advertising and marketing and, with a similar increase in the property market, estate agency. Similar developments also took place in the USA under Reagan's deregulation of Wall Street. The employment gaps in these sectors were filled with young, often single men, sometimes graduates, and always hungry to gain get-rich-quick solutions in an economy otherwise plagued by unemployment and uncertainty following the OPEC crisis and the recession of the late 1970s.

Secondly, more socially, these sectors were in turn equally exploited and exploiting of the situation. Advertising, marketing and image-making, as growth areas in themselves, and as increasingly high priorities in furiously competitive markets, had knock-on, if unknown, effects on their often young and male employees who were now locked into serious competition within and outside individual companies. Significantly, these sectors, whilst successful in offering opportunities for some, were particularly stringent in their processes of selection, recruitment and promotion. The importance of maintaining or developing the correct corporate identity, in areas of work also increasingly premised upon image marketing (as a means of market specialization and of making competitive edge in already exploding and saturated retail and financial markets), was equally critical for competing companies and, indeed, competing young men. The North American influence of Wall Street – where the corporate power look of the Wall Street shark also came from – was immense, as many financial companies in the UK were either taken over or set up with North American management.

The USA also spawned the development of image manuals and image consultancy – most famously in Molloy's *Dress for Success* (1975) – which are now incorporated into an array of image-centred occupations and industries which seek to advise, guide and reconstruct personal, corporate and even political identities throughout the UK and Europe (Gray, 1995; Spillane, 1993; Wark, 1996). The philosophy underlying such operations is often beguilingly simple: why dress, and do, yourself down when you can dress yourself up to impress? A secondary and decidedly tricky question here, though, is that appearances of success may in fact constitute success itself, or cover up a multitude of sins. In addition, confusion is raised concerning the cost of these makeovers, which are often expensive and encourage high spending, though they are justified as cost effective. What is clear, however, is the escalating sense in which appearances are at least *thought* to play a part in personal and corporate success alike. The question, then, of the extent to which appearances actually *do* play a part in success is, in a sense, irrelevant to the growing feeling that they *might*.

Thirdly, underlying these factors were the even more significant trends of rising consumerism and marketing turning their attention to lifestyle advertising. The single status symbols of the 1970s, such as colour TVs and dishwashers, were now giving way to a whole new world of commodity clusters and lifestyle categories. Consequently, to complete fully the lifestyle and looks of corporate power, for example, one not only needed the suit but the braces, the brogues, the shirt, the haircut, the Filofax, the car phone, the car itself, the apartment, the carpets, the decor, the correct entertainments and the appropriate holiday destinations. The costs were colossal and few could afford such luxuries, yet equal expansion of credit cut the cost, at least temporarily. Particularly importantly here, it was the lifting of constraints on financial *consumption* in conjunction with the aforementioned deregulation of financial *production* that facilitated these very high levels of spending inside and outside the City.

Fourthly, politically and ideologically, underlying all of these developments was a move towards individualism and aspirationalism linked to materialism: the view that whatever it was you wanted you could earn it, purchase it and ultimately sell it. As a result, successful masculinity was increasingly defined in monetary and personal terms of possession rather than provision. The implication was that you were what you owned. And this tied in to an additional belief that, no matter what it was you wanted out of life, you could purchase it; in turn, a complete counter-reaction to the spiritualism of the 1960s and 1970s, and a reflection of the increasing commodification of everyday life.

Fifthly, the prime mover of all these developments was demography, as more men now lived alone or were part of a childless partnership, were divorced, or simply sought their independence earlier. This particularly applied to young men as still the most economically productive and most economically secure consumers; for even if their employment was insecure they were still the most likely to seek and find alternatives. The rise in unemployment levels was also coupled with more aspirational developments around masculinity. It was, then, perhaps not surprising that young unemployed men were still spending vast proportions of their limited incomes on looking good or in keeping up in appearances if not in practice.

In total, what these developments added up to was a series of new markets for masculinity. From Gillette to Next and from Tie Rack to GQ, the stage was set for a quite unprecedented expansion in the concept and practice of men's fashion and accessories. It is no coincidence and no accident, therefore, that it was the 1980s which saw the expansion of haute couture or designer fashion for men, or Hepworths turning into Next, or the rise of multiple specialists to take over from department stores, or the launch of men's style magazines, or the rise of advertising targeting men, or men starting seriously to wear suits again, or cut their hair short. It is also, perhaps, no accident that rates of male anorexia have risen, or that cosmetic surgery for men is on the increase, or that men in their millions have started to work out at the gym (Brooke, 1996; Goodwin, 1996; Wolf, 1991). In sum, there is less a purely social change in these developments in men's fashion and masculinity than an adaptation to a primarily economic precedent.

This perspective contrasts sharply with some forms of feminism which have sought to emphasize the importance of sexual politics as part of the cause as well as the impact of these processes (see Chapman, 1988; Moore, 1988; Wolf, 1991). In particular, it is asserted that masculinity has necessarily had to reinvent itself as part of men's response to feminism or, to put it more simply, men have had to find another way of asserting gender dominance. In addition, it is also pointed out that feminist academia has provided the conceptual tools through which these processes of development are analysed. This secondary point is indeed valid, as evidenced in the various citations involved, using directly or indirectly feminist or feminist-influenced theories and ideas including textual analysis and constructionist theory. To claim, though, that feminism has formed the entire canon of criticism used in analysing men's fashion or male narcissism is to ignore the influence of other areas such as gay studies, media studies or, perhaps more importantly, Marxism.

It is also somewhat contentious to assert that masculinity was, or is, in 'crisis', and even if it is, that this is the result of feminism as opposed to other and wider developments such as unemployment. More particularly (as previously discussed) the reconstructions of masculinity invoked in the concepts, representations and practices of consumerism in the 1980s demonstrate very few signs of post-feminist consciousness and many more indications of intensely sexualized and phallocentric muscularity. Some other forms of feminism or feminist perspectives, however, clearly make these wider points themselves (see, for example: Ash and Wilson, 1992; Ash and Wright, 1988; Wilson, 1985).

In sum, then, whilst feminism constitutes an important ingredient in the melting-pot of the concept and practice of men's fashion, masculinity and narcissism, it is certainly not the only one. The precise impact of the phenomenon of the New Man on narcissism is, though, unknown on at least two counts: firstly, as it is too soon to know and secondly, as most research is directed into its hypothetical, if nefarious, impacts upon sexual politics. However, the *potential* of these developments to disrupt not only conceptions of masculinity, but some of the most fundamental premises of contemporary society concerning work, production and modes of living, remains immense.

In the final section, I wish to consider the advertising for Levi's 501 jeans as an analysis demonstrating many of the points I have already made.

Imaging masculinity: unfastening Levi's 501 advertising

> Like so much else about masculinity, images of men, founded on such multiple instabilities, are such a strain. Looked at but pretending not to be, still yet asserting movement, phallic but weedy – there is seldom anything easy about such imagery. (Dyer, 1989, p. 206)

The advertising campaigns for Levi's 501 jeans have attracted significant attention, not least for their unprecedented economic success. They constitute a multi-million international money market in themselves, dominating the entire market for similar products, and are constantly and variously reconstructed as the one and only pair of jeans in terms of a multiplicity of treatments, colours and types, all with the same essential design. Often imitated and frequently copied, undercut, and sold as fakes, they constitute *the* fashion success of the twentieth century.

As a consequence of all of this, their associated advertising has gained serious attention across media, marketing and academic circles alike (Barthel, 1992; Chapman and Rutherford, 1988; Mort, 1996; Pumphrey, 1989; Simpson, 1994, 1996). A consensus or story has developed since to explain their success, essentially told as follows. At the end of the 1970s and in the early 1980s, the jeans market was increasingly saturated and so diverse that nearly everyone of every age, class or area had a pair. In particular, so the story goes, Levi's were losing their market share. The solution lay in a semi-legitimate reclamation of authenticity: Levi's as the original and longest-lasting jeans, also mythologized by 1950s Hollywood icons including Marlon Brando and James Dean. Significantly, this was not the end of the story and the two earliest campaigns, namely 'bath' and 'launderette', were blatantly sexual, as barely clad and glamorous young men were caught in the act of getting their jeans body-clinging wet or unbuttoning them oh-so-slowly in the launderette. This led, not surprisingly, to a serious case of product fetishism as 'it was the display of the product through the product that was sexy' (Mort, 1988, p. 201). The button-flies were critical as constant attention was drawn to accentuated male genital anatomy, an idea played upon previously in the gay community. Given the gimmickry and the simultaneous appeal to authenticity and sexuality, success was not surprising. Levi's now have something of a cult following, whilst the soft-core, prick-teasing advertising campaigns maintain their grip on the market, as in the recent example of 'accident' where a casualty nurse with quivering lips is forced to unfasten the flies of a hunky young man.

Following such media and academic attention, it is perhaps worth examining the elements of these points in more detail. Firstly, it is commonly asserted that authenticity was critical to the success of the advertising campaigns: the claim was that Levi's 501 was the oldest style of jeans and therefore the original, and all the others were either fakes or copies – which was, of course, only partially true, as 501 jeans underwent numerous modifications in design since their inception in the late nineteenth century. This is of secondary importance as it hardly mattered whether the claim was true or not, for it remained an important part of the marketing campaign and, in implication, an equally important part of its success. But whilst authenticity may form a major part of the *justification* for purchase, I suspect its importance in *motivation*, or indeed in *stimulation*, of desire and interest, is a lot less.

This leads on to the second factor: that of the sexuality, or perhaps simply sexiness, of the advertising campaigns. This is a rather underplayed point eslsewhere, as sex is a common and well-known tool in any marketer's kit, used to sell everything from glamorous cars and ice-cream through direct associations to, a lot less directly, cans of paint (where connotations of silk are often invoked). But the sexuality of the adverts is worth some consideration. An initial point of contention here concerns quite where the sexiness comes from, for as much of it would seem to come from the (often very physically attractive) characters as from the frequently off-camera product – from the wearer as opposed to what is worn. The wearer is male rather than female despite the manufacture of 501s for females as well. This has been seen as a significant case of role-reversal in the viewer–viewee relationship, particularly when, as was the case with the first advertisements, the male is seen alone or is constructed directly as the looked-at gender. There is some variation here however as, over twenty adverts later, scenes have involved significant use of female models alone and in interaction with the male model or his jeans.

Thirdly, there is a consistency of attention to the details of the product and, in particular, the flies. This is the factor which, I think, constructs the sexiness of the adverts: the accentuation of the look/don't look and see/don't see configuration. In this sense, the Levi's adverts are oddly conservative and, strictly speaking, very phallocentric as the model's cock is constantly hinted at and yet only momentarily glimpsed *through the product*, a point explored more fully in Frank Mort's work (Mort, 1988). In particular, it is the fact that we are *not* entirely allowed to look at the male that reinforces the construction of the female as the still all too looked-at gender. The difficulty here, though, is that the distinction is still undermined as it remains the male who is the overt focal point, off-set with the defensive phallocentrism of his overall representation. This is similarly a constant issue in pornography as male genital anatomy wholly fails to live up to its phallic connotations and ends up supported through other factors including muscularity, masculine dress including uniforms and denims, and the masculine activities and environment of the outdoors, locker rooms, gyms, showers or workshops (see Edwards, 1994).

This leads on to the fourth point that, despite all the disputes, the adverts do constitute an example of the reconstruction of masculinity through looking, through sexuality, and through consumption. The actual patterns of consumption in this case, though, are rather mixed up, as Levi's 501 jeans, whilst still high sellers overall, have a particular appeal for students as well as other fashion-conscious youth groups and, most importantly, a near mythic appeal for the gay male community. Many young, and some older, men, straight or gay, now refuse to wear anything else and Levi's 501s jeans have gained a status that is as cultist and specific as it is diluted and general.

A final, and often neglected, point is that this development of product fetishism has accompanied a simultaneous fixation with physical appearances and, in particular, a muscular physique (Triggs, 1992). The hunky young guy guided sexily into and out of the flies of his 501s is, without exception, a white, clean-cut, decidedly mesomorphic model. It is, I think, a mistake to try to separate these points of dress and physique, for they not only mutually complement and enhance one another, they are fundamentally mutually *dependent* upon one another, as we cannot, yet, look at a man in other than phallocentric terms. To put it more simply, if he was not a defensively heterosexual and aggressively muscular hunk, we could not look at him at all, as masculinity itself would be called into question for the artificial and phallocentric construction it is. In conclusion, we are increasingly asked to not *see* masculinity, rather to *image-ine* masculinity, and this is the process of imaging masculinity.

Conclusion: private investigations

> The equalisation that men are becoming subjected to in the sphere of consumption is not in the least the equality we might dream of, the equality of free and self-determining beings in free and self-determining association with one another. It is the equality, rather, of self-absorbed yet emotionally anxious personalities for sale. (Wernick, 1987, p. 295)

Throughout this chapter, I have stressed the importance of the increasing pervasiveness of particularly self-conscious or narcissistic representations of men's fashion and masculinity. Importantly, whilst these representations are expanding in quantity, they are narrowing in form and type, as we are increasingly presented with images of young, white and muscular men sporting looks of corporate power or outdoor virility. Contemporary images of masculinity, whilst perhaps a little more diverse, still develop primarily along similar lines and axioms, as the waif, for example, is precisely a waif for what he is not, namely a muscular hunk. As a consequence of this, the same implicit as well as explicit representation of masculinity as sexy, muscular and well dressed is constantly reinforced.

The increasing pervasiveness of these representations is, I think, in itself the outcome of wider contemporary and historical developments in the 1980s, loosely typified as part of wider processes in consumer society, including the increasing emphasis placed upon consumption, individualism and image cultures as a means of specialization in saturated retail and financial sectors. All of these factors have equally had, and continue to have, an impact upon the production and consumption of men's fashion at all levels of society.

It is easy to dismiss some of this discussion as dated and overly centred on the developments of the 1980s; yet in the 1990s, whilst unstructured, velvet and linen looks have overtaken pinstripes and power dressing, the emphasis placed upon men's appearances remains immense, men's style magazines have grown significantly in market terms, and interest in men's fashion has survived the recession and is increasing once again.[8] It is, perhaps, simply too soon to know the private impact of these very public developments, yet the potential to promote anxiety, pressurize relationships and disrupt individual identities and lives, even the economy, seems worryingly unregulated and uncontrolled.[9] As Hollywood stars are required to remove their shirts and top male models are required to work out, or as executives consider their looks for corporate success and young men aim to gain muscles, masculinity is no longer simply an essence or an issue of what you do, it's how you look.[10]

Notes

1. Athena is a major UK retailer of posters, postcards and similar stationery, famous for its products featuring naked men and especially Spencer Rowell's 'L'Enfant' which features a muscular hunk stripped to the waist and wearing only jeans, yet seated holding a young baby: the poster remains their best seller.
2. The primary example of this was Rowena Chapman and Jonathan Rutherford's *Male Order* which came out of a conference on sexual politics (Chapman and Rutherford, 1988).
3. The connections of postmodernity and the New Man are developed in Moore, 1988.
4. The term homosociality refers to patterns of non-sexual relationships and personal friendships amongst men and was developed in the work of Eve Kosofsky Sedgwick (Sedgwick, 1985, 1990, 1993). The concept of social space is a rapidly expanding term used to refer to a particular group's use of specific locations to maintain or develop its interests or identities, for example gay cruising areas or informal ethnic ghettos (see,

for example, Bell and Valentine, 1995).
5. See my own earlier work for a full exposition of gay male sexualization in the 1970s (Edwards, 1994).
6. See also Cook, 1994.
7. It is also worth noting here that recent studies of adolescents' readings of advertisements have portrayed them as increasingly sophisticated consumers, fully aware of the multiplicity of potential interpretations as well as the often high levels of irony and humour involved (Nava, 1992).
8. See Chapter Four and Chapter Five for evidence on each of these points.
9. These are points explored more fully in Chapter Seven and Chapter Eight.
10. There is, of course, a sense in which masculinity was always at least partly premised upon appearances, yet in an increasingly media- and image-driven society where traditional productive and work roles for men are also undermined, the emphasis on appearance must increase, and does so relentlessly.

4

The Marketing of Masculinities

It is the primary purpose of this chapter to demonstrate how the marketing of menswear and men's fashion forms the marketing of masculinities. Prior to this, though, it is necessary to define and unpack marketing theory and practice and how this then impacts upon men's fashion. The evidence for this discussion is premised almost entirely upon interpretation of Mintel, Euromonitor and similar surveys plus some marketing textbooks.[1]

Marketing theory and practice

> Marketing is the management process responsible for identifying, anticipating and satisfying customer requirements profitably.[2]

Marketing is simultaneously a new phenomenon and one which is difficult to clearly differentiate from older forms of selling. It is traditionally defined according to the increasing attention paid to the needs of customers prior to promotion, or even production, of the commodities in question. Historically, it is also asserted that a marketing orientation of making what will sell has, of necessity, taken over from a sales orientation of selling what is already made, as customers are increasingly knowing and markets for commodities themselves are more competitive. Neither perspective, apparently, is concerned with production for its own sake, as this is seen to have disappeared with the Victorians. In addition, it is difficult to separate such interdependent elements quite so clearly, particularly in contemporary society. The difficulty also concerns the degree of emphasis still placed upon the profit motive or, to put it another way, is marketing simply more effective selling?

Marketers, who often market marketing itself as much as the commodities, tend to highlight the centrality of the marketer's concerns with the consumer's needs *prior* to development and promotion of products, the importance of marketing *research* and the *investigative* nature of its practice. Perhaps more importantly, marketing is still generally perceived as a more complex and more multidimensional phenomenon that involves issues of promotion, advertising and presentation as well as the pricing and placing issues traditionally associated with selling. An important point to make here, though, is that the effects of the economy upon marketing are immense and, in times of recession or slump in particular, marketing departments are the first to suffer cuts and market research often ranks as a very low priority despite its potential importance in predicting promotional outcomes. This seems to imply that the underlying rationale of most companies remains one of production and sales with marketing primarily used merely as an aid to more effective sales and profit development. Marketing is then promptly dropped when excess monies dry up. In particular, the more far-reaching potential of marketing, in terms of truly tailoring production according to consumption, remains underdeveloped and perhaps even actively undermined.

The fortunes of marketing have varied historically. Marketing arose primarily after the Second World War following its development in the United States where, to all intents and purposes, it originated. The 1960s and 1970s in the UK saw marketing develop primarily alongside more traditional forms of selling and as a concern for large corporations developing and expanding increasingly complex and diverse lines of products. Small and even medium-sized companies were essentially excluded as they lacked sufficient funds to invest in marketing, as opposed to selling, which was still seen as more direct and cost effective. However, it was in the 1980s that the face of marketing rapidly started to alter and every company from major to minor now sought the expertise of marketers in making production and sales alike more effective.

In particular, it was the expansion not only of marketing departments but of entire marketing organizations that appeared to spearhead developments in the 1980s. Underlying all of this, though, was the wider deregulation of financial services and the City, and it was the service industries – most infamously the utilities – that now sought marketing expertise. At its peak, no one and nothing was exempt from the influence of marketing.

Marketing is easily confused, though, with wider questions of image management and use of the media industries socially and politically as well as financially. The reality was that marketing itself was hit hard following the financial crash of 1989 and the attendant recession. Many (particularly small to medium-sized) companies were forced to close marketing departments. Meanwhile, the pressures placed on marketers in large corporations to produce results increased immensely, particularly in the wake of increased use of independent consultancies. As a consequence, it is not marketing itself, but the marketing consultancy, as a low-cost and insecure operation, which remains the lasting success of the 1980s.

The primary and continuing concept and methodology of marketing is the marketing mix, otherwise known as 'the four Ps' of product, price, promotion and place. Product refers quite clearly to the product in question, its design, nature, specification and market salience; whilst price primarily refers to the means of price-setting and whether other incentives such as price-cuts or discounts are used. Promotion applies to all forms of promotional activity from advertising to personal selling, packaging and PR; whilst place is in a sense a misnomer for distribution or the management of supply and wholesale in an increasingly complex international arena. Effective marketing, therefore, rests on successful 'mixing' of these four sets of factors, often in the context of the marketing environment.

The marketing environment is in turn defined in shorthand terms as PEST. This is an acronym for the following factors: Political (government legislation, trade regulations and social policy), Economic (boom/slump, interest and exchange rates, inflation, income and employment), Social (attitudes, lifestyles, demography, gender, ethnicity and environmental concerns), and Technological (computing, new product development, information technology). In addition, a fifth category of Ecological factors is often incorporated into these models, as environmental concerns have started to have an impact at all levels, from company decisions to consumer perceptions of the product. Despite the apparent contradictions of mass consumption and environmental concerns, ecological factors are increasingly used to sell products, particularly in relation to toiletries and fashion: as seen, for example, in the marketing campaigns of The Body Shop or Benetton. These PEST(E) factors and the marketing mix are then cross-referenced to produce a more refined analysis of a company's or product's market position.

As time has passed, marketing practices have increased in their complexity. Particularly importantly, the development of more psychographic, as opposed to demographic, marketing techniques has led to the now infamous formation of lifestyle categories. Here, groups' and individuals' patterns of consumption are marked out according to far more vague and mixed factors such as attitudes, domestic practices and leisure activities, as opposed to the traditional demographic factors of age, sex, class, area, occupation, and so on. For example, McCann-Erikson, one of the most important lifestyle scales, separates 'Avant Guardians' who are well educated and self-righteous, from 'Self-Admirers' who are young, intolerant and concerned with appearances, from 'Pontificators' who are older, traditional and concerned with keeping order. The tendency towards stereotyping is clearly apparent, yet the success of these scales in allowing companies to target groups and individuals more effectively and promote products through far more sophisticated techniques is equally evident (see for example, Armstrong, 1996). Contemporary advertising, for example, now almost completely depends upon such categories.

Significantly, what is at stake here is product personality, an almost anthropomorphic connection of product with a type of person where, for example, BMWs become loaded with associations of success, sexiness, virility and even masculinity, whilst smaller Renaults are endlessly sold as French, flirtatious and feminine. The more insidious issue here is the commodification of personality which ensues: you are the car you drive and, therefore, without the car you are not 'you', a dangerous situation of dependency and a contentious question to which I wish to return later in the chapter. It is first necessary to document some of the main elements of the marketing of men's fashion in the UK.

The market for men's fashion

Fashion operates to a fast-moving but fixed timetable which influences its marketing. There are essentially two product cycles, complementing autumn/winter and spring/summer catwalk collections, which force a twice-yearly total turnover of stock – thus necessitating the January and July sales which are of crucial significance for fashion retailing, particularly in recession. The product life cycle is of necessity short (though not as short as for fast-moving consumer goods such as food; and there is also much continuation of lines across cycles). In addition, the world of fashion is, of course, notoriously fickle and linked up to individual, social and sometimes unconscious questions of taste, making predictions and promotions particularly difficult, especially as for many people most of the time fashion is not considered a necessity. Price elasticity, referring to fluctuations in demand according to price levels, is therefore an important and associated factor for marketing. Another is that fashion, in terms of its production and consumption alike, is an increasingly and overwhelming international concern with materials and manufacturing, wholesale and retail, often separated and spread across different parts of the world.

In relation to men's fashion, the application of such matrices clearly varies according to the product in question, and the marketing of designer suits is quite different from a value-pack of underwear. However, the underlying principles tend to remain the same. The primary principle impacting upon the marketing of men's fashion is the fickle nature of the phenomenon of fashion itself. As a consequence, fashion goods are often marketed according to precedent, that is to say according to the tried and trusted. Advertising of designer clothing in glossy, stylized up-market magazines or use of direct mail to previous customers are examples of the targeted nature of much fashion promotion in aiming new products at those already purchasing such products. In particular, cracking open new markets in the world of often conservative male consumers who dislike upsetting the applecart of stoic and preconceived ideas of their appearance is particularly tricky. Consequently, the marketing of men's fashion is often highly specialized and segmented according to perceived types of consumers, a point I will explore more later.

In practical terms, the menswear market is primarily divided into two areas of outerwear and underwear. Outerwear refers to suits, jackets, coats, knitwear and trousers; whilst underwear refers to shirts, ties, socks and underwear itself. The former are often seen as more directly fashion-influenced and luxury goods that are purchased less often, whilst the latter are usually seen as routine essentials. There are distinctions within this, though, as suits, formal jackets and trousers often constitute a necessity for office workers; whilst underwear, in the widest sense, is now often seen in similarly fashion-conscious terms from Tie Rack to Calvin Klein. Expenditure on men's outerwear and underwear does, however, follow expected patterns of price and necessity as underwear, in the specific sense, plus shirts and socks form the most commonly purchased items; whilst trousers, jackets and suits are sold less frequently and often as replacements; similarly, coats of all sorts form the smallest market of all. Also, not surprisingly, the market for imports in all forms has increased as the twentieth century has progressed, as has the exporting of fashion goods.

Expenditure according to socio-economic group is also predictable. ABC1 men aged between twenty-five and forty form the major corpus of suit buyers and are high spenders generally, whilst teenagers generate huge spending on jeans and fashion outfits. Not surprisingly, the unemployed and elderly in particular tend to spend least on their appearance, while lower socio-economic groups consume many smaller items such as shirts and trousers in high quantities. As a result, the market for menswear is in many ways similar to the market for womenswear, although the importance of socio-economic position is often more specific in its impact upon men's consumption of fashion.

The market for menswear and men's fashion does differ, however, from the market for womenswear and women's fashion in several important respects. Firstly, the market for men's fashion is traditionally more income-elastic than the market for women's fashion; that is to say, demand for it varies more according to income. More importantly, assessment of men's disposable incomes is particularly critical as single or married men with no children and middle-class incomes are prime targets for marketers, as their expenditure on fashion outstrips other groups often several fold.

Moreover, this then links up with the second point that the market for men's fashion has a tradition of heightened sensitivity to economic conditions including unemployment, recession and economic uncertainty, due to the primacy of men's incomes in terms of family provision and other economic commitments and the lesser importance placed upon men's appearances. This is perhaps changing, though, under the impact of women's increasing employment and personal expenditure. In particular, the rise of working women with significant personal incomes has led to some parallels in marketing of fashion goods for men and women. For example, the expansion of designer-influenced fashion outlets like Next has also had a significant impact, particularly on the promotion of fashion, for women as well as men, since the 1980s.

Thirdly, the product life cycle for men's fashion is usually longer than for women's fashion, as a given style or commodity will tend to have a more extended life expectancy. The product life cycle itself is usually seen to approximate a normal or bell-shaped distributive curve from introduction through stages of growth, maturity and decline to termination. In relation to fashion, though, this is often highly condensed, as many products pass through the process at unprecedented speed or never proceed past introduction. In relation to men's fashion, this factor was also seriously undermined from the 1980s onwards as fashion cycles for men's fashion speeded up markedly; whilst the cycles for women's fashions, spinning still faster, levelled off onto a somewhat 'postmodern' plateau of pastiche and parody of the past. For example, the sexy 'suits and stripes' power look for men in the mid to late 1980s essentially only lasted approximately five years; whereas the prior lounge-suit look of the office had existed with few variations since the Second World War.

Fourthly, women remain important purchasers and consumer's of men's fashion, whereas men do not consume women's fashion in the same way. Women are more likely to wear men's clothes and are, in particular, likely to purchase men's clothes for them, although this applies far more to smaller items like underwear, shirts and sweaters. Whilst men do purchase women's clothes as presents, this is often a practice limited to smaller items and, in particular, with the exception of transvestism, men do not wear women's clothes to nearly the same extent that women wear men's clothes. The reasons for this seem centred partly upon the greater difficulties of making women's clothes fit men physically and, perhaps more importantly, upon the immense stigma associated with men wearing women's clothing other than in entertainment or partying where the practice is mercilessly parodied.

Fifthly, multiple specialists such as Next or the Burton Group form a more important part of the consumption of men's fashion, whereas department stores and mail order tend to dominate more for women. More importantly, men's fashion is often more specialized and directly targeted than women's, which remains more diverse despite economic centralization in relation to all fashion consumption. The precise processes and implications of market segmentation for men's fashion are considered in the next section.

Retailing masculinity in the UK

The primary aim of this section is to unpack the present market for menswear and men's fashion in the UK in more detailed terms. It is important to point out that the market for fashion goods is unusually dynamic and unsettled. Statistical analyses are also prone to inaccuracies due to the rapid turnover of outlets as well as merchandise, difficulties in defining goods and the market, and the multiplicity of ways in which statistics are compiled, mixed and matched. As a result, what follows is a highly simplified and somewhat sweeping and speculative map of the market for menswear in the UK.

In relation to retailing, chain stores and multiple specialists possess something of a monopoly in the market for men's fashion. In particular, Marks & Spencer are far and away the market leader, accounting for up to one in three of all purchases of menswear; whilst the Burton Group, comprised of Principles, Top Man, Burton's Menswear and several sports stores, represents one in five of all menswear purchases. Other multiple specialists such as Next and River Island form significant and growing minority shares of the market, though they are still dwarfed by Marks & Spencer and the Burton Group. The particular success of these companies primarily lies with their size and their longevity as the largest and oldest of menswear retailers.

Marks & Spencer has its origins in the rise of department-store shopping in the late nineteenth century and its postwar as well as early high-street success lay in its appeal to the mass market of family consumers requiring easily afforded and quality commodities. The company also formed a reputation for preferential treatment of staff in the otherwise poor working conditions that have continued to dominate the retail trade. It did not start to encounter difficulties until the 1980s when the increasing media attention paid to design led to some criticism of its conservatism and the lack of style-consciousness in its clothing. The incorporation of new management and a design consultancy, including the leading English menswear designer Paul Smith, has led to a new, up-market appeal to Marks & Spencer's stores, offering somewhat more stylish clothing with the same quality though rather higher prices. Consumers appear prepared to pay the higher prices (despite fewer credit options, as credit cards are not accepted except for the Marks & Spencer store card) and the company has maintained its share of the menswear market. Indeed, it shows some signs of increasing its market share, not least through its total domination of the market for men's underwear. More importantly, perhaps, similar chain outlets and department stores, such as British Home Stores in particular, are also seeing an up-turn in their fortunes in the 1990s as the recession has led to a shake-out from the market of smaller, independent companies.

The Burton Group's past lies in expansion of more specialist tailoring for men. Lord Montague Burton was one of the central founders of men's 'off-the-peg' or ready-to-wear suits in the early twentieth century, and Burton's reputation for mass-produced suits and appropriate cheap tailoring for the rising ranks of service or office workers formed the focus of its success until the 1970s. An increasing emphasis on casual clothing for men in general, and the growth of a youth market in particular, then started to force a reconsideration of the company's position.

In addition, it was and is the factor of identity which accounted for the success, and failure, of the Burton Group. As Frank Mort pointed out, Burton's success in the immediate postwar period lay in its appeal to a 'gentlemanly ideal', a store where men mixed with other men to the exclusion of women to enjoy solid tailoring at low prices, infusing the market of the rising ranks of office workers with a sense of their own self-worth and aspirationalism not entirely dissimilar to Next's appeal to the same group in the 1980s (Mort, 1996, p. 137). With the invasion of casual clothing, the teenage revolution and growing demand for off-the-peg fashion as opposed to tailoring, Burton's has found itself increasingly lost.

Its primary response was, and what is more still is, one of market segmentation. Top Man, a style-conscious store aimed primarily at the youth market, was launched successfully in 1978, whilst Principles for Men (the group's answer to Next) and Champion (a chain of specialist sports stores) were launched later in the 1980s and have expanded in terms of outlets almost continuously ever since. Also incorporated into this strategy was the Burton Group's buy-out of Debenhams in 1985 and the increasing use of in-store segmentation so that stores are either combined, or sub-stores, as is common in Debenhams, are created. The difficulty of this strategy, despite the potential of diversification and the cost-cutting measures of segmentation, is the loss of identity for the Group which now appears as a pale imitation of many of its rivals. This has led to a levelling off, if not a fall, in sales.

The difficulty for men's fashion until the 1980s was the immense gap that separated design-led specialist outlets delivering high-quality, high-design goods at often very high prices to very particular customers with immense incomes, from the utterly tiresome mass-production of often completely designless, if sometimes quality, goods sold through department stores and retail chain outlets. In short, if you wanted style at a price you could afford, you were lost. That is, until Next came along. Next itself is considered in detail later in this chapter. The important point to make here, though, is that Next's impact upon the market for men's fashion was, and still is, immense in terms of the myriad of its imitators from Principles, Oakland and River Island to Bradleys and Blazer, all opened up with varying degrees of success as answers for the affluent rather than wealthy, style-conscious consumer. Mail order, including the Next Directory, and factory outlets also continue to form a rapidly developing market for men's fashion. Design-led independents such as those found on New Bond Street or Savile Row, despite their much-vaunted success in the mid to late 1980s, remain minority and specialist outlets.

The additional point to make here is that the increasing status of designer fashions since the 1980s has also led to a diffusion of the designer influence outside of specialist outlets. For example, major department stores such as Selfridges feature fairly wide ranges of designer fashions. The more important factor though was the rise of imitations of designer fashion, whether in the form of fake products at cut prices or in the near copies often sold in high-street stores. This process was partly facilitated through advances in technology which now allowed not only rapid photographic copy of collections in the press, but rapid production of imitations in the high street.

These processes have led to a separation of Savile Row and similar made-to-measure or individual tailoring firms, from the expansion of 'prêt-a-porter' Armani suits (for example) at equally high prices; and a simultaneous *diffusion* of such designer fashions through fakes, copies and designer-styled products in chain stores. Interestingly, though, Savile Row, having undergone the recession and severe competition, is now shifting away from its more conservative image in favour of a more design-influenced initiative (Falconer, 1996). The primary development of the 1980s was not, then, merely designer-fashion, although the influence of this was immense, but rather the expansion of a new market of mid-range and designer-*influenced* men's fashion that sought to fill the open gap of mass-market and styleless chain stores on the one hand, and high status and vastly over-priced selective design outlets on the other.

As it stands, then, the market for men's fashion tends to fall into four areas as illustrated in Table One. It is, I hope, immediately clear that these four types of outlet are constructed according to their use of the marketing mix and not simply in relation to the commodities they sell. There is significant overlap in the types of products that are sold and also, to some degree, a congruence in the prices at which they are sold.

This illustration starts to demonstrate not only the nature of the marketing of men's fashion, but moreover the marketing of masculinity itself, for all of these four types of outlets, not to mention the variations within them, market their products according to a quite specific type of consumer or personality. Type A stores primarily tend to target men with very high incomes, often executive, creative or City workers and/or those who are single, gay or without children; whilst Type B outlets quite self-consciously market themselves according to age and socio-economic group or, more precisely, twenty-five to forty-year-olds in classes ABC1;

Table One: The Market for Men's Fashion in the UK

	Product	Price	Promotion	Place
Type A	Designer labels, high quality	High, with few offers or discounts	Exclusivity, direct mail, magazine advertising	Large cities, selective affluent areas
Type B	Design-influenced, higher quality, style-conscious	Mid-range, some incentives, store accounts	Less-is-more stores, mail order, direct mailing	Most major cities, high streets and shopping malls
Type C	Mass-produced, design secondary	Low to mid-range, many incentives	Value for money	Prevalence, almost everywhere
Type D	Street fashion, poor quality, style-conscious	Low	Shop window promotions, price cuts, music	High streets, cities, youth culture areas

Type A: Up-market and independent companies, with one or few outlets specializing in designer wear or with their own tailor-made brand, emphasizing quality, design and selectivity, targeted at wealthy and style-conscious men with high disposable incomes, e.g. New Bond Street, Savile Row, Jaeger, Cecil Gee, and up-market department stores including Harrods.

Type B: Mid-market, often independent companies, with own design-influenced, trademark outlets in most major cities, aimed at fashion-conscious affluent 25–40 group in particular, e.g. Next, Oakland, Austin Reed, The Suit Company, Principles, The Gap, and French Connection. Also includes more up-market variants in mail order such as the Next Directory, Racing Green, and Lands End.

Type C: Low- to mid-market mass-produced goods sold in chain stores, department stores and lower-grade mail order, emphasize value for money, market themselves for families, e.g. Littlewoods, BhS, Marks & Spencer, Burtons, Fosters, Cotton Traders.

Type D: Low end of market, mass-produced goods targeted at fashion-conscious youth market, many price incentives and poor imitations of more up-market styles, e.g. Top Man, market and street stalls, Mister Byrite, Milletts, jeans stores.

Type C stores aspire to attract the conservative and income-sensitive family man; whilst lastly, Type D outlets tend to target the young, single and frequently black or Asian.

Masculinity is also marketed though product styles, promotional activities and store design as well as simple pricing. Consequently, Type A stores frequently offer a miniature, specialist and design-conscious environment, copied to some extent in the 'less-is-more' stores of Type B outlets; whilst Type C stores often echo the conservative functionality of their clothes and Type D outlets often play loud pop music in environments not dissimilar to warehouses or darkened nightclubs, thereby excluding all but the young and trendy. Similarly, smaller outlets such as French Connection with its European associations, The Gap with its up-market casual youth appeal, and Benetton with its often controversial political correctness, often have equally striking identities as stores and commodities alike (Horsham, 1996).

This marketing can then start to impact upon one's sense of identity or personality. Consequently, to purchase one's suits at Next is to say 'I am affluent and I aspire to a lifestyle that reflects my success', whilst to consume one's suits at Top Man is to say 'I am young, I am single, and I live for the moment', and to buy one's jeans at Burton's is to say 'I am a family man and value for money is important to me'. This may seem extreme and yet there is little else to explain quite why we are put off from entering one store and tempted to try another when differentials in price or product type, as opposed to product style or the store itself, are frequently minimal. This also highlights the further point that store design is now seen as central to retailing success and many companies, particularly those aiming at more style-conscious groups, make huge expenditures upon store design.

It is important to point out, however, that specific companies and stores do not necessarily occupy the same position over time. For example, Marks & Spencer has tended to move up from Type C to Type B with the developments of the 1980s whilst Next, which spearheaded the same developments so successfully, has started to move from Type B to a B/C boundary position. These 'movers' are not the only important motivators of change as certain other outlets, which I shall choose to call 'oscillators', slide across or even occupy several categories at once. These include River Island and Ciro Citterio, which hover between Types B and D, and The Suit Company which, as a primary example of specialist niche marketing, meanders across all four categories at once. Exceptions to the whole classification scheme include sports stores and specialist outlets, such as specific workwear or leisure wear manufacturers including hunting, fishing and shooting outlets, as well as horse-riding or horse-racing clothing companies. Some of these clearly do not fall within the arena of men's fashion yet the increasing incorporation of 'country and gentry' into 'yuppie and city' centred lifestyles is significant.

From this discussion of the marketing and retailing of men's fashion, certain factors emerge as significant. Firstly, men's fashion is marketed differently from women's fashion and, in particular, it is more specifically targeted at highly defined types of consumer. This is in many ways due to the nature of the market for men's fashion in its sensitivity to outside, economic factors and the conservatism of men themselves. Secondly, and connected to this, these factors are then tied to definitions of masculinity as the selling of men's fashion crucially depends upon the marketing of masculinity. Men as consumers are traditionally more reluctant than women to look into the mirror and require significant reassurance of the safety of such an activity. The heavy reliance on key factors of work-related aspirationalism and heterosexuality in the promotion of men's fashion reflects this, particularly in the case of men's style magazines and advertising generally, as does the personality-typing of the differing types of outlets. Thirdly, whilst many of these factors may also apply to the marketing of fashion for women and femininity, the wider range of products involved there, including a colossal accessories and cosmetics market, combined with the traditional acceptability of female narcissism or interest in fashion, means that the market for women's fashion is greater, more resilient, more open and, in a sense, more kaleidoscopic as opposed to specific. Fourthly, these gendered and sexual differentials in the world of fashion are increasingly slippery, primarily as men's fashion is now marketed more according to its homoeroticism, particularly in style magazines for men like *GQ*, and women's fashion now shares some of the work-related and aspirational marketing aimed at men (see Chapter Five). In addition, the opening up of a series of mid-market, style-conscious fashions for men and women created a sex-commonality not present previously.

The final, and fifth, point is that whilst the market for women's fashion and all that is tied up with it still swallows the male market whole several times over, the *potential* of the market for men's fashion to expand and its *capacity* to grow into one of the leading markets of the twenty-first century is immense and only just opening up, with all the positive and negative consequences that this implies in terms of its impact upon men themselves, the economy and the society as a whole. It is also a market that is currently uncontrolled in formal terms, either economically or politically, and is a primary example of the deregulated excesses of Thatcherism, a potentially disastrous scenario considered in more detail in Chapter Eight. At this point, though, I wish to present a detailed study of the development of Next PLC as perhaps the most successful example of men's fashion in the 1980s.

Male to order: a case study of Next For Men

> The chain was most strongly associated with the revival of the suit and its cultural symbolism. The 'double-breasted look' – slightly exaggerated shoulders, loose fitting, full jacket in shades of navy, grey or black – became Next's hallmark. After more than a decade of decline 'the suit has staged something of a recovery', observed the *Financial Times* in 1987. And, as the paper noted, the move back to formality registered a shift in social attitudes. Younger men were not only 'style conscious', they had also become more culturally 'conservative'. (Mort, 1996, p. 123)

The success of Next, though significant in itself, is also an indicator of a certain shift in perception and representations of masculinity, and it is the purpose of this section to start to investigate this development. Although now hardly ten years old, Next ranks as the sixth largest outlet for menswear behind the Burton Group, Marks & Spencer, Storehouse (BhS and Blazer), C&A, and Littlewoods. If Next is compared more directly with other multiple specialists, and department or chain stores are excluded, then it ranks second behind only the Burton Group; and if the mail-order Next Directory is included then it rises to a position of market dominance and, of more importance still, it spearheads a still growing area of the market for designer-influenced men's fashion. The key question to ask here is *why*, and for the answer to this we need to consider its history and its use of the marketing mix.

Next's history starts with the failing fortunes of Hepworth's stores, a parallel in the market to the Burton Group, in the early 1980s. It was particularly clear that the market for mass-produced menswear was, if not stagnant, then certainly saturated and in need of an injection of creativity. As outlined previously, a gap in the market was found for more design-conscious clothes at mass-produced prices and Next was launched in 1984 offering more stylish formal and casual wear at prices that matched the upper end of those set in chain and department stores. What is more, with the vision of George Davies, who turned Hepworth's into Next, the clothes were also distinctive in their reinvention of 'classic' styles such as broad, double-breasted suits, pleat-fronted trousers, button-flies and muted colours such as navy, maroon, olive, beige and grey that were markedly different from the designless mass market chain stores and the loud styles of the youth market alike. More casual, as well as more formal, clothing was sold simultaneously creating a whole new 'look' for the affluent office worker who wanted a classic suit for work and equally stylish clothes for the weekend. In addition, credit facilities were set up quickly for the convenience and affordance of this whole new wardrobe of lifestyle.

Next's style crystallized several important and wider cultural developments. Firstly, the emphasis upon classics was linked to a wider cultural concern with authenticity that similarly underlay Levi's advertising campaigns and marked a drive away from the loud and tacky associations of the 1970s. Secondly, Next harnessed the wider issue of lifestyle to its merchandise and was intentionally designed as an all-encompassing shopping concept incorporating accessories as well as clothing, the home and family as well as the individual, and full width of casual as well as formal wear. Thirdly, what was more marked, however, was Next's reconstruction of masculinity. Particularly importantly, the clothes invoked associations of the 1940s in the use of dark, double-breasted suits, plenty of stripes, polo shirts, silk ties, and chinos with button-fly fastenings.

It is easy to interpret this reconstruction of masculinity as a sign of cultural conservatism linked to the rising work ethic of the 1980s, yet it also constituted a conservatism with a twist as the intense sense of style, of looking and feeling, was strongly sexualized, often sensual, and loaded with homoeroticism, as the clothes were not presented on mannequins, they were displayed on posters of handsome young models. Next Man was Athena Man with clothes on, the body beneath the double-breasted suit: muscular, fit and sexually potent. It was this sense of phallic display through the product and its associations that marked Next For Men's success and a shift in conceptions of masculinity. The implication was that dressed in a Next double-breasted suit and tie you could become that man in the poster. This simple shift in the presentation of dress, and the representations of masculinity associated with it, went almost unnoticed at the time and was all the more insidiously effective for this, and yet the transformation did not end here.

Running alongside all of this was the development of less-is-more in-store design to echo the classic, quality and select associations of the products. Shops were frequently decorated in wood with little or no music, muted and simple lighting, and displaying clothing that was purposefully laid out to theme an overall look and not to crowd the customer who felt he was finding something select or unique, echoing the effect of classic authenticity that Davies tried to achieve with his products. Sitings of stores were equally selective in the affluent south-east cities and towns using shopping malls and prime high-street locations. Not to overpower the market, outlets were opened slowly over a two-year period whereupon the Hepworth's chain was closed completely.

It is of primary importance to perceive the timeliness of this development of the Next chain of stores. Not only was a gap in the market located for such products, but there was an appropriate climate for their promotion and development. Approximately five years into Thatcherism, the UK was already well versed in aspirational individualism and style-conscious imitation. As financial markets were deregulated, anybody who wanted to be anybody wanted to be in on the yuppie bandwagon of navy double-breasted suits, braces and boxer shorts at work, and beige chinos, button-flies and trendy knitwear at the weekends – and Next sold it all. What is more, there were an awful lot of aspirational males now working in a myriad of computations of 'financial services'. As a consequence, demand was immense. Ironically, this also had an impact on the financial development of the chain itself as George Davies himself was, ironically, in some ways the epitome of the high-spending tycoon of the 1980s (Mort, 1996).

Demography and technology also had their part to play as more men were now living on their own with higher personal incomes, more men who were with women had no children, and more men had busy lives, mobile phones and Filofaxes from which to order their goods, as the one thing they had less of was time to shop. Not to stop here, Next launched its up-market mail-order Directory in 1988 offering much the same product and aspirational importance as the shop. Next had done their market research, evaluated their market position, and used their marketing mix with devastating success. The use of product diversification was also central in this as Next also launched Next Kids, a line of children's clothing, Next Interiors for home furnishings, and later a Next Basics brochure for casual wear.

Difficulties arrived later in the 1980s when sales started to fall flat. Interestingly, the reason was not the recession, but rather technical difficulties with supply and quality of merchandise, coupled with typical 1980s over-investment (Mort, 1996). As the primary example of retail innovation in men's fashion, Next also triggered a counter-attack from both the Burton Group and Marks & Spencer and fuelled a whole host of copy-cats, in terms of commodities and store design, from Oakland and River Island to Bradleys and Blazer. However, despite Next's cultural influence, it is far from taking over the market economically, and its multiple and departmental predecessors have, on the whole, tended to survive its impact, with some costs. In particular, the primary cost for the Burton Group has been its inability to come up with its own solution due to its problematic, if understandable, copy-cat policy.

Perhaps most importantly, the shift in fortunes from the decline of Burton's to the rise of Next has documented a shift in masculinity from Burton's traditional tailoring for the aspiring young gentleman to Next's classics-with-a-hint-of-style and plenty of yuppie aspirationalism. Marks & Spencer's ability and power to employ the likes of Paul Smith has compounded its position as market leader to a point where it now seems so insurmountable as to be without question. The question is raised rather more as to the future of the design-influenced multiple specialist market that Next has created, and much centres on developments in technology and home shopping, in which Next already has a strong footing, and in the market for an ageing population, which Next has yet to conquer as the over-forties still shop and spend, in their millions, at Marks & Spencer.

Conclusion: marketing masculinities

In conclusion, I have structured this chapter according to an analysis of the marketing of men's fashion as the marketing of masculinities. In many ways, this discussion reflects the wider processes of consumer society, particularly in the 1980s. The trend towards designer wear and designer stores, the emphasis upon lifestyle, the targeting of the affluent consumer, and the diffusion of fashion across local, cultural and international lines all reflect the same, or similar, developments in the wider, consumer society. Also central in all of this is a certain shift in conceptions of masculinity, particularly around the axiom of style and aspirationalism. What is missing from this analysis, though, is a sense of the meaning of these developments for the consumer, which I start to explore in the next chapter.

Notes

1. See Bohdanowicz and Clamp, 1994; Brown, 1995; Chartered Institute of Marketing, 1993; Key Note Report, 1987; Mintel, 1987, 1989; Retail Business, 1980, 1983, 1987, 1988; Retail Intelligence, 1994.

2. This is the definition used by the Chartered Institute of Marketing in teaching and training. Of significance here is the use of the word 'profitably' and those involved in marketing are often ambivalent about its inclusion. The definition does illustrate, however, the importance of analysis of markets *prior* to production of goods as well as the centrality of the customer.

5

Consuming Masculinities:
Style, Content and Men's Magazines

Men's magazines in the UK now constitute a growth market. But the so-called new style magazines for men are not new internationally and, in the UK, men's general interest magazines have an equally long history. It is, to put it simply, that they weren't *called* men's magazines and this is what constitutes the key difference: the self-conscious targeting of men as consumers of magazines designed to *interest* men if not necessarily to be *about* men. They were and, what is more, still are called car magazines, hi-fi magazines, sport magazines, and so on; in short, magazine journalism which quite clearly targets men's interests without targeting men themselves.

To expand upon some of these points in turn: firstly, in North America and some European countries, particularly France, men's style magazines have a long if far more limited history, similar to style magazines aimed at women. For example, *GQ* and *Esquire* in North America have existed since at least the Second World War and so, similarly, has *Vogue Hommes* in France. Secondly, there is an equally historic legacy of men's interest magazines as opposed to men's style magazines in the UK and yet over ten years ago you could not have purchased a single men's style magazine or even a men's general interest magazine. As I write in 1996, there are six monthly style titles with a total circulation of upwards of 500,000 and increasing monthly, plus several biannual fashion manuals, making the UK something of a world leader in terms of men's style titles (Driscoll, 1995). There is also a new series of style-influenced titles that concentrate on other issues such as health or sport in particular yet persistently dip their toes into issues of men's style.

As a result, then, there are three sorts of men's magazines: the first is a list of fully style-conscious and self-conscious general interest magazines aimed directly and overtly at a male readership including *GQ*, *Esquire*, *Arena*, *For Him Magazine* (*FHM*), *Loaded* and *Maxim*; the second, a series of supposedly more specific periodicals with a more open readership that carry regular features concerning men's style and fashion including *Attitude*, *i-D*, *The Face*, *The Clothes Show Magazine*, *XL* and *Men's Health*; and the third, a gargantuan group of men's interest magazines which covertly target men as their primary readership including car, computing, photographic, sport and technical titles. Due to the concentration of this current text on men's fashion, the first and to some extent second groups are clearly of most relevance. However, I do not wish to exclude entirely consideration of other areas, particularly in terms of the contextual development of men's style magazines.

The contextual development of men's style magazines

The most interesting question concerning the so-called new crop of men's style magazines in the UK is, why now? When men are apparently more concerned with their economic survival than ever, why do they apparently respond so positively to such an initiative and why have marketers of such products thought it fit to take the risk? The answers to these questions are, I think, complex yet quite concretely located in the social, economic and political changes of the past ten to fifteen years. Firstly, economically, whilst many men have suffered financially it is also clear that others have advanced. In particular, young white, well-educated and middle-class men are still the primary employment group for professional and primary sector work. This connects up with a second, social and demographic factor that as more men now live alone or do not have children, some men have also seen increases in their personal incomes. Thirdly, and more politically, Thatcherism and Majorism in the UK have seen an equal encouragement of individualism and aspirationalism, in turn a key factor in men's style magazines and one which I wish to expand upon shortly. Fourthly, it is also argued that men are increasingly encouraged towards self-awareness via the impacts of the women's movements and gay movements which have equally challenged hegemonic notions of heterosexual masculinity. Yet lastly, and most significantly of all I think, it has become more socially acceptable for men to be consumers *per se* and, more importantly, to be consumers of their own masculinity or, in short, to look at themselves and other men as objects of desire to be bought and sold or imitated and copied. At least *some* male narcissism is now socially approved.

The difficulty concerns locating quite where this development has come from. It is easy to see feminism as the primary cause of male self-reflection, and yet I would question the logic of such a notion for there is often little evidence to suggest traditional heterosexual male practices have altered at all in relation to the home, workplace or sexual relationships. What has perhaps shifted is the perception rather than the practice of male sexuality itself as something more artificial and floating, as opposed to natural and fixed.

The linking factor of significance here is the rise of a visible and partially more socially acceptable gay masculinity. Gay men, supposedly free from the hang-ups of heterosexual masculinity concerning the stereotypes of effeminacy associated with style-conscious consumption, have in many ways acted as a pilot consumer group for men in general. Gay men's relation to consumption does differ from heterosexual men's primarily on two counts: they tend to have fewer financial commitments and therefore often higher disposable incomes; and their consumption patterns are often used to reinforce their sexual orientation, whether through spending the pink pound or in maintaining a distinctive lifestyle or identity, and fashion is often quoted as an important example of this. It could, perhaps, also be argued that they have in turn become the bridge by which marketers have made inroads into mainstream heterosexual masculinity. This position is however easily overstated and leads to a series of negative and nonsensical stereotypes as explored further in Chapter Seven. But those affluent and high-spending gay men who *have* spent and consumed in a way of which marketers had previously merely dreamed, have also provided the template and take-off point for exploring consumer masculinity in general. As a result, gay sexuality remains a significant, if often unacknowledged, factor in the development of men's style magazines targeting men and masculinity.

An underlying factor of importance in all of this, though, is the development of style magazines themselves. These currently include such titles as *i-D*, *Details* and, most importantly, *The Face*, all of which developed in the early to mid-1980s to cater for the tastes of the young, affluent, style-conscious and the often city- as well as self-centred youth cultures, set around strong interests in music, dance and night life. Of particular concern here were the links with pop music, particularly the New Romanticism of groups such as Spandau Ballet and ABC as well as early Blitz nightclub culture; and the rise of lifestyle itself in concept and practice, a primary example in the UK coming in the form of Habitat. This high-style, mid-price household chain store turned coffee mugs and tea trays, let alone sofas and furnishings, into fashion accessories in the 1960s and all over again in the 1980s.

The development of style magazines for men has had two significant effects. It created a style cultural intelligentsia of experts disseminating their specialist know-how on matters of appearance, a point picked up on recently in Frank Mort's work (Mort, 1996).[1] More significantly, though, it led to an immense emphasis upon consumption as a means to join the new style elite: wear the right suit, visit the right store, get seen in the right places in the right apparel (as whatever the 'wrong' apparel was or was not, it was always the cheaper option). What all this added up to was the primary (though still nearly always missed academically) role of men's style magazines in encouraging and perpetuating high spending. This, I would argue, is the foremost function of these magazines.

As a result of all of these elements, masculinity became a lifestyle commodity to be bought, sold, admired through retailers' windows and aspired to in style magazines, just like anything else. However, it is to the question of a specific style and content of men's magazines to which I now turn in the next section.

The style and content of men's magazines

The style and content of the new so-called men's magazines appears, initially, varied and free-floating, yet I wish to assert in this section that the style and content of these titles is in fact quite extraordinarily fixed, apart from the superficial construction of what one could call product personality.

The first point to make concerning this new crop of men's style and general interest titles is that they are all, without exception, relatively expensive. Priced currently from £2 to £3 per issue, it is patently clear that we are not talking of competition with *Woman's Weekly*! The counterparts for women would more realistically include such titles as *Vogue* and *Vanity Fair*, if not *Tatler* and *Harpers & Queens*. As a consequence, despite any pretence to the contrary, all such titles clearly most directly appeal to affluent, professional or managerial men in socio-economic groups ABC1 and not to factory workers, mechanics or drop-outs. (The appeal of *Loaded* is more contradictory and a point I will explore shortly.) Market reports from two of the leaders, *GQ* and *Esquire*, also make it clear that this is quite overtly their target market.[2] The one exception to this rule is that students clearly make up a significant part of the readership (according to the same reports). The important point to make here, of course, is that students ultimately form the next generation of affluent professionals.

A second point to make is that, with the exception of *Attitude* as a more directly gay-oriented title, they all assert the heterosexuality of their readers, often with a near-defensive vengeance. This is the most significant and contradictory point to make, for if affluent and professional gay men constitute a major target style-consuming group with money to spend and fewer hang-ups in doing so, then why do such titles tend to exclude and, on occasions, even directly offend their non-heterosexual readers? The answer would seem to be the high level of anxiety relating to the exclusion of heterosexual readers if homosexuality is too overtly or openly condoned. This does not explain, though, why such titles cannot apparently occupy a neutral or open territory of unspecified sexuality. The explanation, I suspect, lies in the felt necessity of off-setting the near-pornographic and homoerotic nature of much of the imagery used to advertise products or illustrate features on fashion and style, which varies from the phallic and sculpted to the soft-focused and artistic (see Plate Four). In this sense these titles do covertly cater for their gay readers, although this also tends to fetishize and delegitimize homosexuality.

A third area of overlap concerns the overt legitimation of consumption itself as a socially acceptable leisure activity for men and as a symbolic part of a successful lifestyle. This is not only reflected in the high profile and level of advertising itself, it is also seen in the constant textual and visual attention paid to commodities and products as part of a material aspirationalism from clothes and accessories to cars and technology. A connected, and I think significant, factor is the implication that this then leads to the increasing construction of masculinity according to commodities. In other words, you are the man you are due to the cut of your suit, the cost of your hi-fi or the car you own. What this then leads to ultimately is masculinity as a matter of how one looks and not what one does, a point explored previously in Chapter Three.

This leads me on to the fourth and key point of aspirationalism. Even the style-defensive *Loaded* still espouses the pleasures of spending, the good life and looking sharp, whilst the others routinely define successful masculinity in terms of money equally conspicuously earned and spent. This is in many ways part of the overall 1980s trend towards lifestyle advertising along aspirational lines. As a result, these titles (quite didactically on occasions) inform their readers of the significance of fine tailoring, the glamour and sexiness of suits, ties and all the accessories, give instruction on casual correctness, and advise of the fundamental importance of personal appearance to success and even to personal security. This is not, I hasten to add, confined to suits, ties and accessories (although the never-ending concern with these items is a source of some fascination in itself), but spreads to cover toiletries, physique, cars, technology and even property. Most importantly, the stirring up of anxieties, all-consuming dreams, desires and allures is quite dazzling and only satisfied in equally endless spending.

Lastly, all these titles implicitly depend upon a city as opposed to a rural or even suburban milieu, both in terms of the products and services advertised only being accessible in big metropolitan cities and particularly London, and also in relation to the fast-lane lifestyles they promote. In sum, what these five points add up to, then, is a quite specific and often fixed targeting of single, affluent, city-dwelling, high-earning and high-spending, primarily heterosexual men to the exclusion of all others: that is, all those who do not at least aspire to this way of living or its values. As a result, what advertisers in these titles tend to tap into is a semi-conscious daydreaming state where fantasies of self-image are of paramount importance (see Bowlby, 1993; Campbell, 1992; Radner, 1995).

From New Man to New Lad: analysing men's magazines

New Lads are just as much a 'phony' marketing phenomenon as New Men. (Simpson, 1996, p. 249)

This section focuses on a content analysis of the so-called 'new' men's magazines as defined in the introduction to this chapter. In particular, I wish to refer to the content of four of the market leaders: *GQ*, *Esquire*, *Arena* and *For Him Magazine*. These are the most established and, as yet, biggest or most solid sellers in the market for men's style magazines. In addition, I also wish to consider the two newcomers, *Loaded* and *Maxim*, for which circulation figures are as yet unconfirmed.

GQ or *Gentlemen's Quarterly*, launched in the UK in 1988, is essentially the English version of its long-running North American counterpart, set up under the directorship of the American editorial entrepreneur Michael VerMeulen. *Arena* is the longest-running men's style magazine in the UK, started in 1986 under the editorship of Nik Logan, seeking product diversification following the international success of *The Face* magazine and similar in kind to *Details* in the USA. *Arena Homme Plus* is a biannual and additional fashion label bible based on *Vogue Hommes* in France, and was started successfully in 1994. *Esquire*, like *GQ*, was launched slightly later in the UK in 1991 as a counterpart to its highly successful equivalent in the USA. *For Him Magazine* is a corporate product of the magazine conglomerate EMAP in the UK and was launched initially under the simple title of *For Him* in 1985. *Loaded* was sprung in Spring 1994 and *Maxim*, the most recent of all the titles, had its premier edition in April 1995. Neither of these titles seems as yet to have an international parallel. *Attitude*, interestingly marketed as the magazine for real men, was launched in 1994 in the UK as a gay-oriented, if not gay-exclusive, style title (and as an alternative to the news-oriented *Gay Times*), similar in kind to *Genre* or *Out* in the USA.

The method of content analysis was very simple and intentionally quite unsophisticated as it is the widest and most general features which are of interest here. Recent editions of all the titles were taken and analysed according to the space they devoted to differing forms of content. Firstly, advertising content was distinguished from editorial features in the magazines. This is, in fact, not the hard and fast distinction it may seem as many of the editorial features, particularly those in relation to fashion and lifestyle, have an implicit advertisement intention giving listings, stockists and prices for the items pictured and discussed. Secondly, categories were then created within these two groups according to easily recognized, overall definitions of the content involved. From this, ten central categories were devised to cover all of the features in the magazines, although not all the magazines ran features in all categories. The pages devoted to the categories were then totalled and converted into percentages of the entire magazine including front covers. Circulation figures were derived from media information packs received from the magazines themselves upon request and compiled using ABC readership survey statistics. The results were then put into chart form as presented in Table Two: A Content Analysis of Men's Magazines.

From this simplistic analysis, certain points are immediately apparent as important. The advertising content in all cases is significant and, at its highest, reflects the up-market, style-conscious and glossy emphasis of the titles concerned. *GQ*, *Arena* and *For Him Magazine*, as the most self-consciously style centred of all the titles, have the highest figures here; and one may well expect the two lowest, *Loaded* and *Maxim*, to increase their advertising revenues as they increase their market significance. Within this and with the exception of *Loaded*, advertising for fashion, and its related accessories such as aftershaves and jewellery, wipes the floor with all other categories of advertising, taking up to a quarter of the entire content of the magazine. (*Loaded*'s low showing in this category is due to its advertising concentration upon the arts and, in particular, rock music, explained in terms of its ex-music-journalist editorship and editorial.)

In editorial, the fashion and lifestyle features category also tends to dwarf the others in most cases, again taking up to nearly a quarter of the entire text. It is also of significance here that the same three magazines which have the most advertising in this area, *GQ*, *Arena* and *FHM*, also have the three highest rates in the equivalent features category, creating a situation where nearly 50 per cent of these titles are concerned with fashion, lifestyle and accessories.

Certain titles display a particularly strong emphasis in specific categories. *Esquire*, for example, has the highest concentration of features on serious issues, reflecting its general interest rather than style-conscious focus; whilst *Loaded* and *Maxim* have a far higher joint emphasis on the arts and interviews than the others. This reflects their somewhat anti-style conscious opposition to the other four titles and is also part of a more working-class emphasis, in the loosest sense, as the arts mentioned are rock, pop music and cinema rather than classical music, opera and theatre. They are also, though, the most grossly (hetero)sexist of the six, featuring the highest use of features on women and sex. *Maxim* in particular runs up to three times as many features here as the others. The other four in fact have a certain tendency to run one, near soft-core pornographic feature on sex or women which often seems set up in defensive opposition to the endlessly homoerotic displays of men's fashion, style and accessories. This is particularly the case with *GQ* and *FHM*, as *Arena* is rather more serious in its addressing of such issues and includes some, minor attention to gay sexuality. Apart from interviews with a variety of famous faces, all other categories gain

Table Two: A Content Analysis of Men's Magazines

	GQ	Esquire	Arena	FHM	Loaded	Maxim
Circulation	110/80	97/65	80/68	60/60	–	–
Editor	Michael VerMeulen	Rosie Boycott	Kathryn Flett	Mike Soutar	James Brown	Gill Hudson
Price	£2.40	£2.40	£2.40	£2.50	£2.00	£2.50
Advertising:	34	24	35	33	25	19
Fashion	25	15	23	23	11	8
Technology	4	5	4	5	1	6
Alcohol/Tobacco	3	2	6	4	2	3
Other	2	2	2	1	11	2
Features:	66	76	65	67	75	81
Listings	7	4	8	5	9	5
Lifestyle, etc.	24	20	21	21	13	13
Sport	5	2	7	2	7	5
Health/Fitness	3	10	1	4	0	6
Sex/Women	1	0	6	5	10	15
General/Arts	5	15	10	12	15	20
Travel	4	5	0	0	2	3
Issues	5	11	2	2	0	6
Fiction	3	1	0	0	0	3
Interviews	9	8	13	11	19	3
Surveys	0	0	0	2	0	2
Total	100	100	100	100	100	100

Note:
Results based on May 1995 editions.
Circulation figures for 1994/1991, in thousands.
All other figures given in percentages.

minor coverage, which makes the final point that, despite all pretences to the contrary, these are all in some way up-market titles strongly concerned with the self-conscious marketing and consumption of masculinity and narcissism employed in heavy uses of advertising and features on fashion, lifestyle and appearance. The peacock is indeed on parade, at least within the pages of these style titles. This also leads perhaps to the assumption that these titles perform an implicit function of reinforcing a style culture which does not in reality actually exist, adding some weight to similar discussion of women's magazines acting as escapist outlets (Craik, 1994; Radner, 1995; Winship, 1987).

Within all of this though there are, as I have already mentioned, minor variations particularly in what one might call product personality. In particular, each of the titles concerned expresses a quite distinct set of characteristics or values which, most importantly, centres on a particular construction of masculinity or personality. For example, *GQ* nicknames itself as the magazine for men with an IQ and features extensive coverage of executive concerns from quality tailoring to property and corporate spending. More than anything else though, *GQ* represents the interests of the notorious yuppie, or the suit-wearing, swaggering, and narcissistic lover of money. Similarly, *Esquire*, whilst appealing to exactly the same socio-economic group, applies an anti-narcissistic, quintessentially English attention to detail and quality, eschewing issues of style in favour of general and often quite conservative interest. *Arena*, as an off-cut of *The Face*, sneers equally at such conservatism and asserts a counter-cultural art student's sense of elitist style that most men could not and, what is more, would not afford. It was hardly surprising, then, that it was *Arena* who launched the biannual *Arena Homme Plus*, an unashamedly design-centred and haute couture-focused fashion manual for the label obsessed. In a sense, *FHM*, although usually the loss-leader of the four, is the most honest as a directly and self-consciously narcissistic style-centred glossy that takes little interest in worldly affairs, flogs free samples, and appeals to men who are still Brylcreem boys at heart. One would also say that there is something rather laddish about it were it not for *Loaded*, best described as a bargain bible for lager louts, being concerned with beer swilling, shagging and looking sharp, or simply being objectionable, and often in that order. It is the most ambiguous of all the titles on offer, at once ironic and blindingly reactionary. In particular, it is tempting to see *Loaded* as the sarcastic equivalent of the BBC TV programme *Men Behaving Badly* but whilst the latter is clearly intended to be funny, *Loaded* is all too easily taken seriously by those who don't know better which, incidentally, is the magazine's trade mark.[3] *Maxim* is a less extreme variation on the same theme, with an unashamedly post-feminist or primordial viewpoint on sexual politics (depending on how you look at it), including a guide to getting a rich wife.

It would seem, then, that as the most recent additions to the list, *Loaded* and *Maxim* have equally set themselves up as the laddish and supposedly more down-to-earth opposition to the high-flown narcissism of some of the others, though this usually ends up in some kind of working-class machismo or undiluted misogyny. Interestingly, the success of *Loaded* has led other titles to drift increasingly towards using New Laddism, as opposed to narcissistic New Mannism, as a means of selling magazines. As a consequence, there is an increasing use of semi-naked women, frequently on the front cover, and many an article on stag-night antics. In particular, *GQ* and *Arena*, as previously the least gratuitously sexist of all the titles, now endlessly splash topless models amongst the advertising for designer suits; whilst *For Him Magazine*, desperately seeking increased circulation, sells free glimpses of the new Pirelli calendar and incorporates a separate letters page specifically for stories of lager-induced urinating accidents! As a result, the recent and reactionary drift of men's style magazines is increasingly giving cause for concern.[4]

In amongst all of this, there are in each case some genuine and serious attempts to inform and educate men, not only in relation to fashion and spending, but also in quite coherent and intelligent advice concerning health, money and sexual relationships. Whilst not progressive, then, even at their worst these titles do not misinform or actively promote violence and discrimination. The question of their exact intention, though, and in particular their relationship to men's fashion, is discussed in the next section.

Interpretations and intentions

Tim Edwards: What are the main aims, would you say, of most men's style magazines?

Michael VerMeulen: Entertain readers. Deliver readers to advertisers. In that respect, it's the same as any magazine. (Interview, January, 1995)

More academically, interpretations of men's style magazines, like many such developments of the 1980s, have tended to emerge around the theme of the New Man. The self-conscious style magazine for men was seen as the outcome of wider developments in sexual politics increasingly encouraging men to look at themselves and other men *as men* or, more simply, as the product of a redefinition of masculinity in terms of narcissism (Chapman and Rutherford, 1988; Mort, 1986, 1988, 1996; Nixon, 1993). Academic attention has tended to centre on the question of the interpretation of images of masculinity presented in these titles. In particular, much attention has focused on the late Ray Petri's work with *The Face* and other titles in constructing representations of heavy-lipped and pouting young men, often of mixed race, in particular. Such attention, whilst of significance of and to itself, has had the deleterious, if unintended, effect of reinforcing a frankly ridiculous notion that such representations – which are entirely unrepresentative of the overall presentation of masculinity in men's style magazines – constitute some kind of radical shift in the construction of masculinity; when the reality, as I have already asserted, was and still is far more conservative and linked to the fostering of an aspirational and narcissistic masculinity that makes money for the fashion and media industries alike (see also Chapter Three).

In light of the prior commentary, then, it is perhaps more accurate to see men's style magazines primarily as vehicles for a new 'all-consuming' form of masculinity, encouraging men to spend time and money on developing consumer-oriented attitudes and practices from shopping to leisure activities and to enjoy their own masculinity: in short, a narcissistic and particularly introspective set of primarily auto-erotic pleasures. Men's style magazines have very little to do with sexual politics and a lot more to do with new markets for the constant reconstruction of masculinity through consumption: buy this to be that; own a double-breasted suit, portable CD player or BMW and be a man! If men's style magazines respond to anything in sexual politics then it is the undermining of definitions of masculinity in terms of production or traditional work roles, and a deep-seated set of anxieties concerning the lack of future focus for young men, which has almost nothing to do with reactions to second-wave feminism and almost everything to do with the fear of unemployment. Reactions to second-wave feminism, whenever apparent, take one of two forms: disinterest or defensiveness. There is therefore little progressive here in terms of sexual politics, though a lot in terms of the shifting terrain and sands of masculinity.

The New Man has also received added nails in his coffin from the development of the New Lad, a counter-reaction if ever there was one (Margolis, 1995). Where the New Man was caring and sharing, if overly concerned with the cut of his Calvin Kleins, the New Lad is selfish, loutish and inconsiderate to a point of infantile smelliness. He likes drinking, football and fucking and in that order of preference. Yet despite all the sneering at the perceived effeminacy of the New Man, the New Lad is oddly still all too self-conscious and quick to consider the cut of his jeans or the Lacoste label on his T-shirt: in short, he is that most ghastly of all configurations, defensively working class which also means defensively masculine. The link with style-conscious football is unsurprising here as football has historically always been a bastion of blow-drying, suit-swaggering, sharp-looking English laddism. In common, then, with other fads and fancies, he has his origins in other areas, namely pop music and the rise and rise of fashionable football where loutishness has become elevated to an art form. For example, one only has to think of Eric Cantona who, successfully convicted of a violent offence, was *still* hailed as a hero; and Britpop, where the scruffy, badly behaved and derivative heroes of Blur, Oasis and Pulp are now being used to sell the latest designer labels. Herein, however, also lies the irony, for there is as much continuity as there is change in the development of New Laddism. If the New Man sold muscles and scent, Armani and Calvin Klein, then the New Lad sells T-shirts and trainers, Hugo by Hugo Boss and Prada. As a result, the styles may have altered, yet the drive to consume remains the same (Simpson, 1996).

I raised the question of the exact intention of men's style magazines in several face-to-face interviews with some of their editors, which were conducted in early 1995. From these, a series of points emerged as particularly important. Firstly, developments in the economy and in social attitudes were cited as equally and mutually influential in the rise of interest in men's fashion, and the expansion of men's style magazines and retailing attendant with it – whether in relation to the fluidity of income or the social acceptance of design-consciousness. In particular, in relation to the rise of men's fashion in concept and practice, economic deregulation or democratization of income and the increased status of designer garments were seen as equally significant. Secondly, the centrality of a certain socio-economic group of high-earning and high-spending single men was seen as vital in fuelling these overall developments and, more specifically, the role of style-conscious and aspirational professionals was seen as particularly important. Thirdly, there was also an explicit assumption that this group is increasingly sophisticated and knowing in relation to its spending patterns and that this applies to issues of quality as well as style. As a consequence, the didactic or educational as well as entertainment functions of men's style magazines were seen as equally important. For example, explaining the virtues of wool suits over polyester ones was cited as indicative of such didacticism rather than as a ploy for random unmitigated consumption and, as Nick Sullivan, fashion director at *Esquire*, pointed out to me: 'On one level it is about buying, but really it is to make sure the reader spends rightly, or makes the right choices. It's more about *how* to spend it and not to waste it'. This taps into the question, mentioned earlier, of the magazine's creation of a cultural elite. It also raises the issue of the role of men's style magazines in covertly perpetuating spending, often reinforcing the perception of fashion as confusing and complex and, therefore, the consumer as in need of guidance. The increased confusion concerning the casual–formal dividing line in particular was given as an example here, as suit jackets for instance were worn increasingly with jeans, and so on. Fourthly, these trends were also seen as the result of a generational change, as the fathers of the 1960s and 1970s were seen to pass on their sense of style to their sons. The difficulty here concerns accounting for the thousands of fathers and sons who were, and are, entirely disinterested in the issue and, in particular, the role of generational reaction and counter-reaction in creating differing trends in fashion. Finally, and perhaps most importantly, there was a strong, if implicit, sense of the expansion and untapped potential of the whole market for men's fashion, accessories, and perhaps for the consumption of masculinity itself, primarily due to marketers' increased recognition of men's, as opposed to women's, economic dominance and solvency.

Conclusions: consuming masculinities

In conclusion, throughout this chapter I have stressed the importance of the development of a self-conscious and narcissistic masculinity actively promoted in the expansion of the so-called new men's magazines. I have also argued strongly that the rise of these magazines is most easily understood or accounted for in terms of a series of economic and demographic developments including the increasing significance of young, single men with high personal incomes; the impact of sexual political movements such as feminism and gay groups; and, in particular, the advance of an aspirational individualism in concept and practice, promoted politically through Conservative policy and ideology and acted out quite concretely at work as well as in the retail market.

Of critical importance in this, though, is the increasing acceptance of consumption itself as part of masculinity in identity and activity, as more and more men appear prepared to look into the mirror, purchase products for their skin or hair care, or wear a vast array of more fashion-conscious styles of clothes. This is, I think, not as new as it seems, as men in the 1960s and 1970s were concerned with their appearances, reacted against some forms of formalist conservatism in dress, and started to use products such as hairspray and deodorant in ways that only a decade earlier would have had their fathers quaking in their collars and ties. The net result of this is that the rise of a self-conscious or narcissistic New Man was not so much a passing fad as a continuation of a set of developments set in motion after the Second World War; and the advent of a series of up-market glossies designed to complement, cater to and more seriously exploit these developments is not so much a surprise as an expectation. In addition, there is much continuation of all of this in the current fad of the New Lad.

The question to answer, then, is not 'why did it all happen so suddenly?', rather 'why did it all take so long?' The answer would seem related to the very deep reservoirs of anxiety that still attend men's narcissism and sexuality, particularly in England, still a country where men put on a stiff upper lip more readily than a sharp suit or a self-conscious display of their own sexiness. And yet, despite all of this, it is still unequivocally the case that masculinity is increasingly sold, marketed and consumed as part of an overall series of social, economic and political processes that validate male narcissism. The peacock is not, perhaps, on parade yet, though he is certainly taking the first few steps upon the catwalk.

Notes

1. It should be pointed out here that Frank Mort's application of the concept of a style elite is based on Bourdieu's analysis of the role of cultural intermediaries (see Chapter Two). The application is indeed an interesting one as the role of the more up-market style magazines for men in disseminating expertise, in particular, is of profound significance to their construction.

2. I refer here to the media information packs readily supplied by the magazines themselves and based, in turn, on ABC and NRS readership surveys.

3. The trade mark slogan of *Loaded* is in fact 'The magazine for men who should know better'.

4. I am thinking here of Channel 4's *Without Walls* discussion of New Laddism shown in Spring 1996; and of Mark Simpson's recent work (Simpson, 1996).

6

Just Looking: Masculinity and the Contemporary Shopping Experience

In the previous two chapters, I started to unpack important aspects of issues raised in Chapter Three, particularly concerning the role of marketing and consumption in the expansion of men's fashion in the 1980s and the reconstruction of masculinity around the theme of the New Man and, more recently, the New Lad. This has laid a heavy emphasis on the role of advertisers and marketers alike in the production of specific patterns of consumption. Consequently, in this chapter, I wish to start to explore another set of issues which place more emphasis on consumers themselves and their experience of consumption. This will, as we shall see in the last two chapters, also start to raise and develop a new politics centred on consumption. In the first instance, though, we start with one of the most fundamental elements of consumer society, shopping.

Shopping is commonly perceived as the linchpin of consumer society for the whole concept and development of consumerism appears to depend so completely upon its continued practice. Shopping is also often seen as a new or modern phenomenon crucially dependent upon the development and expansion of capitalist consumer society. This is something of a fallacy as shopping, in the sense of the sale and purchase of items, has its origins located more concretely within the processes of market trade that extend into the medieval period and pre-industrial capitalism. What commentators on shopping are commenting upon is in fact the changing nature of the shopping *experience* rather than the nature and development of the whole shopping phenomenon.

This chapter is primarily concerned with the nature and formation of this contemporary notion of the shopping experience. It has, as a consequence, four central sections: the first is a consideration of the history and development of the concept and practice of shopping; the second, a discussion of the contemporary explications of shopping in terms of its experiential importance to the formation of identity; the third, a discussion of the often contradictory nature of the contemporary shopping experience in relation to individual as well as structural causes and effects; and the last, a consideration of masculinity and the contemporary shopping experience. Particular connections with the world of fashion and conceptions of masculinity are also incorporated as appropriate.

Plate One   Front cover of *Arena Homme Plus* no. 3, Spring/Summer 1995.
By kind permission of the editor.

Plate Two Boss by Hugo Boss.
By kind permission of Hugo Boss.

Plate Three From the Austin Reed 'Look the Business' advertising campaign, Spring/Summer 1996.
By kind permission of Austin Reed.

Plate Four From the Canali Autumn/Winter collection 1996.
By kind permission of Canali.

From markets to malls: the historical development of shopping culture

> In the contemporary world, the signifying and celebrating edifice of consumer culture has become the shopping mall which exists in pseudo-democratic twilight zone between reality and a commercially produced fantasy world of commodified goods, images and leisure activities that gratify transformed desire and provide packaged self-images to a distinctive form of subjectivity. (Langman, 1992, p. 40)

As pointed out previously, shopping has its earliest roots in the development of market trade and mercantile culture. Interestingly, this simultaneously locates shopping alongside the development of the fashion industry and within the framework of an exchange of goods and not a crude cash nexus. The development of a specifically capitalist cash culture did, though, start to transform the nature of the shopping experience (Wilson, 1985). In particular, the shift from a simple exchange of goods to paying for commodities in money created a culture that was inherently more acquisitive; not simply in respect of the profit motive, moreover, in relation to the possession of tangible and owned goods in exchange for intangible and earned money. In paying with money one gave up little, other than in economic terms of opportunity costs; one simply added to the pile of possessions.[1] At the centre of this point is, of course, the concept and practice of surplus value as, to put it allegorically, one did not swap two cows for three sheep, one made three sheep's worth of surplus value from the two cows and then kept the two cows as well as the surplus value. (The increasing intangibility of buying, exacerbated by the credit boom, is a point not without implication and one to which I shall return shortly.)

The other most important development was the move from mere individual or small-scale production through to group and mass production and with it the separation of ownership and production. This is, of course, an implicitly Marxist perspective, yet the point remains a simple one: production was increasingly separated from consumption through the expansion of an ownership and exchange system. Whether this then automatically adds up to a two-class society, exploitation and potential revolution is entirely another matter.[2]

The formation of mass production quite clearly still necessitated mass consumption and with it the means to market and sell. In the first instance, this related to the market-place itself, set up simply with minimal personal investment, a practice still thriving today in relation to novelty, charity or small-scale operations. Mass-scale operations implied something altogether different though: the outlet, store or specialized premises for the sale of products: in short, the shop. It was hardly surprising that this development should start in the most affluent parts of the city, or where investment and demand were particularly high; or it should apply initially to the wealthy and middle classes only, whilst the working classes were still confined to markets as consumers as well as traders; or that the earliest stores should show a certain similarity to the market-place, whether as corner shops selling every necessity or as department stores encompassing numerous markets in themselves. All of these developments did indeed take place under the auspices of industrial and financial capitalist expansion in the nineteenth century. Consequently, the high street, or series of specialist shops as we currently know it, is a relatively new invention heavily reliant on capitalist financial expansion, increasing transportation and the development of the city itself (Shields, 1992).

Of primary underlying importance in all of this is the rise of mass consumption coupled with mass production; the involvement of the working classes as consumers, then, remains as critically important as their involvement in production. This is, of course, one of the most common sources of complaint in relation to more orthodox and some more recent forms of Marxism. The point often made is that Marxism has tended to neglect the role of consumption, as a result of the heavy emphasis placed upon the means and/or forces of production as the loci of identity, struggle and development in capitalist society. Importantly, and not coincidentally, this criticism also forms one of the primary assertions of postmodernity theory.[3]

The development of the shopping mall, though, is rather less simply explained. Part of the explanation for its development lies in the demands of consumers themselves, tired of little or no transportation, poor parking, traipsing all over town from shop to shop in all weather conditions, and taking it all home again. The shopping mall therefore offered convenience for some: namely those with the transport, time and money to pay often high prices to support the increasing overhead costs. These are, of course, common criticisms to which I shall return later.

Certain points from this discussion of the history of shopping emerge as significant: firstly, the great ogre of industrial capitalism and the profit motive is not entirely causal of the whole development of the shopping phenomenon and its primary impact has centred on the nature and formation of the shopping experience or perhaps, to put it more simply, how we shop rather than why we shop, though this is a point open to discussion. Secondly, the increasingly common complaint that shopping is a site of inequity – not only in terms of exploitative costs but also in relation to access – is not entirely new. Shopping has a history of inequity as old as the aristocracy, who could access and afford the world's goods in their own homes whilst their working servants lived on their wits in street stalls and markets and, more importantly, mass consumption has never meant mass access. Thirdly, the current concern with the acquisitive and associated cultural value of commodities is also not entirely new and may well have its history located in the development of systems of exchange themselves rather than in many later developments. This is, though, a point I wish to pick up on in the next section for what has, perhaps, altered is not so much shopping itself, rather our experience of it and the meanings attached to it.

I shop therefore I am: shopping and identity

Concepts and catch-phrases such as 'I shop therefore I am', 'shop till you drop' or even 'the shopping experience' appear new and indicative of a very contemporary series of developments. In more academic terms, this is translated into the relationships of shopping and postmodern society, or shopping and late consumer capitalism, also seen as part of the contemporary, cutting edge of society. At the centre of such claims is a series of assertions which I wish to consider in turn. Whether these assertions, taken together, add up to more than the sum of their parts, is a point I wish to explore at the end of this section.

The first and key assertion related to the notion of the changing nature of a particularly contemporary shopping experience concerns the idea that shopping is increasingly a leisure activity and not simply a matter of mundane necessity or utility (Shields, 1992). This assertion rests upon a series of other more empirical points including the fluidity of income and rising living standards, coupled with a declining working week and increasing leisure time, plus the development of supermarket or self-service stores which specifically allow the customer to peruse and inspect as opposed to simply purchase. These points are of themselves contentious, particularly considering the variety and inequity of individual and group shopping experiences in terms of financial and geographical access according to class, occupation, sex, race or age, to mention only a few of the potential variations and sources of discrimination and inequity. It is perhaps simplest to point out, then, that shopping remains a major and increasing source of leisure for certain population groups or individuals.

Secondly, and allied to this, it is also asserted that shopping and consumption are increasingly constitutive of identity, that is to say, people are increasingly defined according to their consumption patterns (Langman, 1992). Increasing support for this assertion comes from the actual marketing of commodities which is centred more and more on complex notions of personality and lifestyle types, as defined in terms of consumption patterns as opposed to simpler notions of socio-economic groups (see Chapter Four). It is also easy to point out that personality is at least partly constituted or reinforced through commodities, particularly those which are clearly apparent or easily recognized including clothing, cars and property. However, these ideas or indeed practices are not entirely new and were formulated academically much earlier in terms of concepts such as commodity fetishism, conspicuous consumption and the separation of content and meaning. Also, those with the most leisure time to consume are often those with the least access or money, such as the unemployed, single parents and the elderly.[4] Particularly contradictorily, it is important to point out that to go shopping does not necessarily mean to go spending and, in this sense, shopping is particularly insidiously constructive of identity as it is the practice of looking, desiring and interacting that is critical, or the simple *process* of shopping itself which is significant. This factor is then connected with the earlier nineteenth century concern with the processes of seeing and being seen, or voyeurism and exhibitionism, that underpinned Walter Benjamin's work on department stores (see Benjamin, 1982).

Thirdly, an underlying and central issue concerns the notion of association and meaning attached to commodities: commodity sign value is seen as increasingly significant and as having overtaken use or utility value (see Baudrillard, 1983). Very importantly, therefore, it is also asserted that purchases are made according to a series of individually idiosyncratic and socially structured values surrounding the goods and not intrinsic to them. This is partly a matter of taste and partly a matter of status, two points put together simply in the idea that 'taste classifies the classifier' (Bourdieu, 1984). But this is again nothing new as goods have given their owners status since the goods themselves were invented, and this was understood academically in terms of a paperchase of social class where people were caught up in processes of imitation and differentiation (Simmel, 1973). An added concern is the allure of advertising and marketing, promotion and packaging, in constructing an essentially artificial significance for the goods affected. The difficulty here is that the consumer is then sometimes seen as a kind of passive dupe operating under false consciousness, a point put most forcefully in the work of the Frankfurt School (see, for example, Adorno and Horkheimer, 1993).

This ties in with the fourth point, though, that the processes of shopping and consumption rest upon the invocation of a whole series of unconscious desires, dreams, and ultimately a psychoanalytic process of unconscious wish fulfilment. This perspective is put most persuasively by Rachel Bowlby in *Shopping with Freud* (1993), where she analyses the whole transaction of viewing, wanting and purchasing goods, or simply consumption, in psychoanalytic terms. The immense problem here though rests upon the implication of a completely empirically unprovable assumption, namely the unconscious. Interestingly, though, she shows how psychoanalytic and marketing discourses have increasingly intermingled during the twentieth century. Appealing and common-sensical as this perspective may seem, this phenomenon is of itself equally explained as the outcome of operating within a post-Freudian world framework of concept, understanding and experience.

A fifth and final point, then, is that shopping is primarily now a subjective experience of image processing, association and value interpretation that is as individual and idiosyncratic as it is social and structured. Given the overwhelming variety of goods on offer to fulfil every need there is some credence for the idea that consumer choice is hardly a simple, rational calculation of utility.[5] Similarly, given increasing access to vast arrays of often near-useless or luxury goods, it is easy to assert a growing concern with values, wants and needs that have very little to do with survival. However, there is some concern as to whether the acquisition of commodities ever was simply a matter of utility value and survival, though it is perhaps also important to assert that the matter of the use*less* value of goods has consistently increased over time, particularly as disposable incomes have risen considerably, at least for some population groups. Porsche cars and designer fashion are prime examples of the stupendous excesses that exist within contemporary consumer society and yet, whilst we may moralize against them, it is precisely their sheer excessiveness that is at the crux of their appeal, for there is no rational justification or cost-conscious sense of quality that explains spending six-figure sums on cars or four-figure sums on items of clothing: the only reason for doing so is it makes you look, and feel, good. It is this sense of excess which at least partly determines the mark-up on the price. For example, in paying £1000 for an Armani suit instead of under £200 for a similar design in Next, one is purchasing a significantly higher quality garment in terms of material, design and finish – but not over 500 per cent superior.

One of the central tensions of the above summary of the contemporary shopping experience is the question of gender. As stated earlier, the consumer was for some time seen primarily as female, whilst the producer was seen essentially as male. This separation of the genders into apparently competing spheres rests upon a series of increasingly outmoded assumptions including the ideas that men work and women do not; that men do not have the time to shop; and, what is more, men do not want to shop. These points are increasingly contentious due to the expansion of 'women's work' coupled with the decline of traditional 'men's work'; the expansion of the means to shop including extended opening hours and mail order; and the increasing social acceptance and indeed promotion of men as consumers in the media and advertising in particular (see Craik, 1994; Mort, 1988; Nixon, 1992; Simpson, 1994; Spencer, 1992).[6]

Importantly, though, these points expose the myths of masculinity and consumption as men have always shopped, only in different ways and for different purposes, such as in shopping for sports and technical equipment from computers to cars and from hi-fi to DIY, and have actively taken part in any major financial decisions as guardians of the cheque account. The tricky question here concerns the notion of a significant increase in men's role as consumers of items previously defined in stereotypically feminine terms and in so-called women-only locations, including food in supermarkets plus clothing and personal accessories in department and similar stores.

The concern here is not the question of men's role in personal shopping, something they quite clearly do take part in, rather the notion that this is a recent or new phenomenon. The primary example of this is the narcissistic New Man, discussed critically in Chapter Three, yet the secondary and prior example is that of the *flâneur* and, even earlier, the late-eighteenth-century dandy, who were equally overt and active consumers of appearances and related products.[7] Studies of late-Victorian masculinity, even, show a consideration of detail and cut in suits and an attention to toilette that radically undercuts any conception of the radical newness of masculine narcissism and, what is more, does some damage to the stereotypical view of the voyeur as male only, for the *flâneur* remains a quintessentially masculine construction. In common-sense terms too, the masculine peacock parades and not the feminine peahen.

All of this tends to create rather an open question concerning quite exactly when and where this contemporary sense of consumption as a primarily feminine activity has come from. Much of the answer depends upon the increasing sense of enforcement of traditional gender roles that took place during the development of Victorian industrial capitalism, particularly at the level of the middle classes, a point picked up on successfully in the work of some early theorists of consumption (Simmel, 1973; Veblen, 1925). This process was perpetuated, and strongly reinforced, following the Second World War in the often quite aggressive marketing of the happy housewife myth in the 1950s, itself part of an oppressive government attempt to force working women to retreat into the home. The development and expansion of the mass media, from magazines to the start of television advertising, also played an enormous role in ramming home, on occasions quite literally, the notion that a woman's place was in shopping for her man who, conversely, was conspicuous by his absence on both counts. This compounded the nineteenth-century notion of the non-working woman as a middle-class asset, and also firmly located the formation of masculine identity outside of the home and, frequently, in the office as opposed to the factory. Consequently, the ideal of the happy housewife in her apron, shopping until she dropped for her hard-working man in a suit at the office, remains a dominant fantasy today, and set up the parameters for defining masculinity and femininity, according to production and consumption respectively, for decades to come.

To pull all of these points apart in turn, though, is perhaps unfair, for if shopping is now primarily a leisure activity (at least for some) and constitutive of identity through a series of socially constructed, subjective, and perhaps exploitative, experiences, then we are indeed considering a whole new and potentially important, if not necessarily 'postmodern', shopping phenomenon. The problem remains, though, the interpretation of this new form of shopping experience which, on closer inspection, appears particularly paradoxical.

The shopping paradox: expression or exploitation?

In the preceding section I discussed the underlying assumptions and prevailing accounts of primarily contemporary theory of the shopping experience. These perspectives state that the contemporary shopping experience is one of expression of personality and that it is an increasing part of the development and perhaps ultimately the dissolution of identity, constitutive of an inner world of psychological desire and need, as well as being an increasingly significant factor in the formation of an image-oriented or representation-oriented society. Consequently, whilst there is some controversy concerning the exact outcome and implications of these developments, there is an implicit assumption that this is the primary or driving logic of the new consumer society. In this section, however, I wish to stress that this is, in fact, only half the story, and that what we are considering is ultimately a shopping paradox.

The other half of the story paints a far less rosy and, indeed, far more ordinary picture. If you ask people if they like shopping or what their experience of it is, the common response is to ask what sort of shopping one means. For many people there is a clear distinction between the credit-card rapture of shopping for clothes and jewellery in glowing shopping malls, or taking trips along quaint alleyways for holiday souvenirs; and the weekly trudge around a supermarket on a rainy afternoon groaning over the rising prices of staple products and negotiating a cramped car-park. Shopping *is* a seductive pleasure-seeking experience for some people some of the time; whilst for many people a lot of the time it is a tiresome chore that has all the excitement of wiping the floor.

It is worth considering at this point, at least hypothetically, what are the primary factors in purchasing fashion or clothing, often seen as the epitome of the more identity-driven aspects of shopping. Take, for example, the case of a man wishing to purchase a new suit, primarily – though perhaps not exclusively – for work purposes. Prior to entering the shop, two factors stand out as of primary importance: firstly, whether the shop is likely to sell the kind of suit required; and secondly, whether the price range is appropriate. Also apparent is a pre-entry sense of what is wanted, or a mental representation, potentially derived from a multitude of sources, including what his peers are wearing, what his partner thinks or may think, what's 'in' at the office, and styles which appeal in magazines or on TV, or were simply seen somewhere previously. On entering a shop, he finds a couple of styles he likes, which are the right price and which he thinks are appropriate for the purpose in mind.

The major issue in the next stage has nothing to do with styles or association and is a question of whether the retailer has the right size and whether it will fit, a factor which has not necessarily improved with the expansion of designer fashion (Levene, 1996). Factors such as the helpfulness of staff and facilities for trying on the clothing and seeing it on also play an important part at this point. Supposing, for the purposes of this discussion, that the shop has each of the styles in the right size and they fit at least fairly well, then a far more subjective and finely tuned set of interpretations comes into play: for example, navy or grey, single- or double-breasted, the feel of the material and, perhaps most importantly, a sixth sense concerning what feels right and gives most pleasure to the touch or to the eye – in short, what suits. He opts for one, pays for it, passes pleasantries with the assistant and leaves, hoping he has made the right decision.

So, while fashion and style are significant in making initial decisions concerning what to try and in final decisions concerning purchase, they are hardly deciding factors in themselves, as the access, price, fit and the sense of appropriateness can wipe out their significance at any one point. There is also a strong sense in which some factors are socially and/or structurally determined: for instance, access to the shop, styles on offer, prices he can afford or not afford, what will or will not suit in the office. In addition, there is a near-unconscious sense of like and dislike, ease or unease, concerning the decisions taken, which is almost limitless in its multi-factorial elements (including the opinions of others, the feel of the material, how something looks on someone he knows, previous experience, etc.) that no amount of store allure or clever marketing or anything else can either know or overcome. In short, one is confronted very directly with the action and structure of shopping for fashion.

Perhaps more importantly, shopping as a contemporary leisure activity is increasingly riven with social divisions according to access, transport and provision and, most simply, money; and many – particularly the elderly, single parents, the poor and the unemployed – do not have the means to partake in a consumer society. A primary paradox here is that those with the most money to spend, namely those in dual income full-time working households, have least time; whilst those with least money, such as the unemployed and the elderly, have hours to kill every day. Shopping, as an activity in itself, is relatively free and the invitation to the isolated, depressed or simply dislocated is consequently colossal. Easy access to credit, and the dislocated sense of not paying that comes from it, opens up particular difficulties for the poor and especially the easily led.

I suspect that an increasing cause of psychological illness is the pressure of living without the means to consume. Some, very limited, evidence for this assertion is provided through the rises in rates of shopping addiction (or shopaholicism) and shoplifting which are often also connected to increases in credit default and debt. It is also provided in the examples of voluntary self-help groups including Lawrence Michaels's 'Wallet Watch' which, with only very limited operations, receives over 1000 calls per year from worried spenders.[8] Reports from the National Association of Citizens' Advice Bureaux, who provide one of the very few examples of free debt counselling as well as links with government Credit Unions, confirm that the problem is expanding and takes up an increasing proportion of all cases and resources. So, whilst for some the contemporary shopping experience is one of pleasure and expression, for others it remains the epitome of misery and exploitation, often added to through inept social policy – points explored in detail in Chapter Eight.

A more complex point concerns the particular nature of the shopping experience of the affluent and pleasure-seeking populations. These groups commonly complain of a lack of variety, at least in the provinces, and a strong sense of limitation and tedium, or a shopping *malaise*, in shopping malls in particular. This is a paradoxical point: as consumer society has expanded and more and more shops have opened up, the sense of restriction of choice has also increased. If we take the example of men's fashion – apparently the epitome of contemporary diffusion and diversity – the sense of tiresome conformity, of the same styles presented in the same ways in the same shops from Plymouth to Edinburgh, borders on the depressing. In addition, the increasing globalization of fashion is also leading to an *international* sense of the same monotony.

Shopping malls are perhaps illustrative of an issue at the very heart of the contemporary shopping experience: identity. They are in a sense space*less*, one feels lost and out of contact, as if entering a post-holocaust zone. It is this sense of the *loss* of self which leads on to the need to *find* self through consumption, whether in window-shopping or in expensive purchasing. The sense of ennui, or even depression, that sets in is not, therefore, the result of utter uniformity but rather the dazzling vacuous display of variety; a quite *existential* sense of confusion as every store mirrors, sometimes literally, oneself. For some, particularly the isolated or depressed, this literally means one has to *buy* something to *be* something. Within this, fashion as the very articulation of 'self-on-the-shelves' is particularly prominent. People are *not* dupes or victims, yet they *are* disempowered.

This leads me on to a critical point of shopping and power: to what extent are we active or passive consumers? We are presented with an increasingly contradictory picture of ourselves as rational actors making choices concerning everything from provisions to pensions, with producers and service-providers tripping over themselves to outwit or outstep us all; and ourselves as cultural dopes, consumed and sucked into something over which we have no control, particularly if we are poor or in some way excluded. What is often invoked here is the notion of consumer choice as a con-trick and an illusion, something we like to think, and what is more they like us to think, we have. But in one sense at least, the choices we have are quite real, for in a supermarket society we can, and do, pick and choose, mix and match, to suit ourselves and our tastes. When presented with endless products that perform the same function for an equivalent cost, we constantly pick on one: someone wins and someone loses. The choice is limited and strings are pulled, yet shopping is a far more complex process than that represented in fictional Stepford.[9] Interestingly, the drama of such films comes precisely from the war of power that ensues and this, I wish to assert, is the nature of the contemporary shopping experience: an un-winning war zone.

Masculinity and the contemporary shopping experience

In the preceding discussion, I have tended to neglect the question of gender in trying to highlight rather than confuse underlying factors of significance, such as historical developments in shopping, social divisions, and the role of the individual consumer. As pointed out previously, the consumer was defined historically as feminine, and if one assumes (I think fairly safely) that this perception is increasingly misplaced and that men *are* increasingly shopping for themselves and others, and that men *are* increasingly involved in all aspects of consumption from traipsing around supermarkets to enjoying the raptures and passions of fashion, then this raises a very salient question concerning the reconstruction of masculinity *through* consumption.

Answers to this question work on several levels. Firstly, in terms of the masculinity equals production, femininity equals consumption matrix, it is important to point out that, even at the supposed peak of its application in the late Victorian era, men did take part in consumption practices, though differently to women, and working-class women in particular played important roles in production. Rather than the confused notion that production and consumption are essentially mutually *opposed*, it is perhaps more accurate to see them as *complementing* one another. For example, in performing a productive role at the office men were, and still are, required simultaneously to consume the appropriate attire, namely the right style of suit and tie, or to adopt certain lifestyles or take part in appropriate leisure activities, particularly in terms of career progression. In addition, production, at least in terms of making money, forms the gateway to consumption and, conversely, consumption in terms of opportunity or possession forms one of the main motivations for work or production. It is ludicrous to assume that, in playing an active productive role, men were excluded from consumption, or vice versa. What is often at issue here is the secondary and associated notions of activity and passivity that construct such a strong sense of gender difference in production and consumption. In particular, it is the perception of the female fashion victim which forms the epitome of the conjunctions of femininity, passivity and consumption. This also helps to explain, at least partly, the suspicion of homosexuality and stereotype of effeminacy that often attends men seen as too interested in their appearance.

Secondly (as we have seen earlier in this chapter and in Chapter One), men have historically often played important roles in more 'passive' or 'feminine' forms of consumption as well, whether as dandies, *flâneurs*, or aristocrats. What we are perhaps witnessing in the late 1980s and 1990s, then, is a contemporary example of a much more historical set of more contradictory and often gendered processes where, across centuries, particular groups of often affluent, young or homosexual men have sporadically courted disapproval to live up to their personal ideals.

Thirdly, as is I think already clear, the relationship of masculinity and consumption in contemporary society is complex, not least of all due to the significance of social divisions. Whilst some affluent and often young men may enjoy and play an important part in the reconstruction of their masculinity through consumption, many poorer, older or inappropriately located men are primarily *constrained* in relation to consumption. In addition, as we shall see in Chapter Seven, patterns of consumption for men differ radically in terms of racial variation and sexual orientation. The contemporary reconstruction of masculinity through consumption, then, is neither without precedent nor as new as it seems, and is a far more limited development than is commonly supposed. The question of its wider impact is, however, raised in Chapter Eight.

Conclusions: just looking

Throughout this chapter I have stressed the importance of shopping as an *experience*. This implicitly accepts and promotes a perspective that sees shopping as a personal and subjective activity as opposed to an objective concrete reality. Consequently, at the crux of this is the role of 'just looking', or window-shopping, supposedly gaining in importance during the twentieth century. A key question is exactly what is happening in window-shopping, and certain factors stand out as significant here. In the first instance, such shopping practice primarily applies to luxury goods, of which fashion forms a primary example, and not so much to staples or the supermarket. Secondly, the expansion of window-shopping is connected primarily to the simultaneous development of shopping malls as climate-controlled and glitzy zones providing acres of shop frontage precisely for voyeuristic purposes. And thirdly, it is also an activity increasingly tied up with the investment of self, as the desire to look, to try, or to decide prior to purchase occurs where the risk to self, financial or psychological, is greatest. It is hardly surprising that stores selling high-status or high-fashion goods are the primary sites of window-shopping, and it is partly the development and expansion of some of these goods themselves which explains the paradoxical nature of the contemporary shopping experience. For example, electrical and technical goods have formed an entire series of markets in themselves, and the sheer variety of everything from shirts to shoes, and from spray-cans to washing powders, dazzles the consumer and forces him or her into endless perusal and inspection of options.

However, I do not wish to imply a simple acceptance of this essentially poststructural perspective, but would query it on several counts. The shopping experience varies according to social and structural positions, divisions and sites of inequity, particularly according to questions of access. In addition, this personal and social side of shopping is not entirely new and has a history that extends back into pre-industrial mercantile capitalism and market trade. Also, as shopping itself has differing meanings for the same people in the same position at different times as, for example, the experience of shopping for staple products is not the same as shopping for personal luxuries. Most importantly, in contemporary perspectives on consumption, shopping is commonly perceived one-sidedly as a source of pleasure and self-expression, particularly in relation to such issues as fashion and personal spending. The processes involved in shopping itself are seen as increasingly constitutive of identity. But this implies that *either* the consumer is an asocial rational actor making choices divorced from all aspects of society, *or* a passive dupe in a system of string-pulling signs and values. The reality, I assert, is paradoxical: shopping is simultaneously a rapturous heaven of self-expression *and* an anxiety-provoking and competitive hell for producers, marketers and consumers alike.

A linked question concerns the significance of men looking at, relating to, or even evaluating other men *as consumers*, as opposed to producers, particularly in relation to fashion and appearance. This raises important issues concerning racial and sexual variation in the role of the *flâneur* and, more widely, men's practices of conspicuous consumption. The importance and potential impact of all of this is considered in more detail in Chapter Seven.

Notes

1. Opportunity cost is the cost of giving up one thing in order to have something else: for example, in spending £250 on a new outfit one pays the opportunity cost of not affording a second holiday. To put it another way, everything has its price in respect of resources yet not necessarily in money.

2. For the Marxist, and particularly the Frankfurt School, this does of course lead precisely to an exploitative class system (for example, see: Adorno and Horkheimer, 1993; Marcuse, 1964).

3. See particularly Baudrillard, 1983; Bauman, 1992; Bourdieu, 1984; Jameson, 1984; Lyotard, 1984.

4. Commodity fetishism is an orthodox Marxist term which refers to the processes of goods gaining the meanings and associations of social relations; conspicuous consumption has since passed into common parlance though was explicated academically by Veblen, 1925; whilst questions of inequity are raised effectively in the work of Cahill, 1994.

5. This is, of course, the classical economic perspective upon consumption where the consumer operates in a world of unlimited needs and wants, with scarce resources, making rational choices.

6. The changing nature of gender relations of work, production and consumption primarily reflects the rise of service and secondary-sector work and the decline of manufacturing and primary-sector occupations, as opposed to any apparent or simple expansion of women in 'men's work' or positions.

7. The figure of the dandy is well known and associated with the excesses of the aristocratic Beau Brummell in the early nineteenth century (Laver, 1968). The *flâneur*, or stroller, refers to a later nineteenth-century construction of masculinity where men, usually in the City, would stroll in smart clothes and not without some conspicuousness through the streets and shops as primarily visual consumers of display (Benjamin, 1982; Tester, 1994). The parallel connections with contemporary concepts of cruising and exhibitionism are clearly apparent and start to undermine the Mulveyesque view of looking relations (Mulvey, 1975).

8. Lawrence Michaels runs a helpline offering counselling for those falling into poverty through over-spending or loss of income. Interestingly, government support is not forthcoming (see Russell, 1994).

9. Stepford is the partly science-fictional and partly real Connecticut town of *The Stepford Wives* and follow-up films, where women were mentally and technically controlled into loving, passive wives through brainwashing by their husbands. They ended up resembling parodies of the bimbo shoppers of Proctor and Gamble commercials, and it is this powerful image of women as supermarket zombies talking about hubby's dinner that sticks, albeit a bit comically, in the feminist and consumer-oriented mind alike.

7

Express Yourself:
The Politics of Dressing Up

In this chapter, I wish to start to explore the politics of fashion in relation to gender, race, sexual orientation and, to a lesser extent, class, focusing on the social movements of the 1960s and similar political developments since. As a result of this, I also hope to show how the differing aspects of the politics of fashion are essentially interconnected: class-driven *and* gendered, racialized *and* sexualized. As the overall focus of this work is on the interconnections of masculinity, fashion and consumer society, these issues are also raised in the final discussion where a consideration of the significance of gay sexuality, visual and style cultures is also presented.

For a long time, fashion has been seen as an apolitical phenomenon, outside of politics, and of little concern to politicians. It is still the case today that politicians rarely involve themselves in decision-making processes that impact on fashion – although the rise in VAT on adult clothing in the UK and the question of its introduction on clothing for children is one exception. (In addition, sales taxes in the US and similar policies in parts of Europe, plus the impact of interest and exchange rates, all have some effect.) Fashion is, however, now a very political phenomenon. This is due, for the most part, to the various social movements of the 1960s and 1970s that sought to politicize appearance as part of an overall politics of identity.

The perception of fashion as an apolitical phenomenon has always been a partial *mis*perception, as fashion and appearance have always played a key part in the politics of difference. The politics of difference here refers to those politics which affect, reinforce or even invent difference within groups and societies whether according to class, age, gender, race, sexual orientation or, more simply, the politics of bodily regulation. For example, sumptuary laws were used periodically – and particularly in the wake of the Reformation and later periods of Puritanism – to regulate perceived extravagance, which usually meant expenditure on personal appearance and fashion. This still persists today in the rather mixed series of attitudes towards fashion, and particularly haute couture, often seen as wasteful, unproductive and superficial. Often what is implied in such attempts to moralize against extravagance is a sense of social, as well as economic, control in maintaining class distinctions, an attempt to stop people 'putting on airs and graces' or 'getting ideas above their station in life'. Sumptuary laws were rarely applied at the top of the social ladder and were aimed primarily at the middle classes as a defensive gesture from the aristocracy (Barnard, 1996).

What is perhaps less apparent in the application of such legislation is the issue of gender. The stereotype of the extravagant and wasteful person spending plenty of time and money on their appearance and fashion was usually a woman. As with most stereotypes, this was not merely the production of myth as middle- and upper-class women *were* the primary consumers of their own or their menfolk's income (see Chapter Two). If women of leisure were often mocked and portrayed as superficial and passive, then men who adopted similar modes of living were condemned with the vitriol of hell-fire and damnation. The primary example of this process at work were the dandies of the early nineteenth century who were seen as excessive, effeminate pansies in need of three years' hard labour (Laver, 1968). This often masked a reality of aristocratic wealth which meant these men did not need to work and, on occasions, a serious attempt to redress the dullness in some areas of men's dress. This sense of unease concerning dressed-up men continues into the present as very well-dressed men, unless pop or film stars, are often seen as narcissistic, silly, homosexual or all three; whilst their female counterparts are perceived as stylish, having good dress sense, and fit for the front cover. However, the situation concerning the interpretation of fashion increased in complexity in the 1960s when the politics of identity entered the scene and crashed the party.

The 1960s represent a rather mythic period in time that is open to misinterpretation. It is particularly apparent that the whole of the UK, France or the USA were not the same as swinging London, Paris or New York, although the seismic effects were felt throughout the countries in question. The difficulty lies in assessing the degree of continuity and change that took place at the time and, within that, the particular groups most affected. The 1960s in many ways represented a continuation rather than a disjunction from the 1950s, as the motors of postwar consumerism continued to accelerate and spread wider throughout society. Thus, in an economic sense, the rise of 1960s hippie and minority fashions followed on from, rather than broke with, the apparent stoicism of the 1950s. This popular perception of stoicism was centred on a notion of fashion as reinforcing a sense of a time when 'men were men and women were women', in other words when men *looked like* men in their sharp, shoulder-widening suits and slick hair-styles, and when women equally *looked like* women with their hour-glass figures, full skirts and high heels.

However, the difficulty with this view is that although the gender differences in men's and women's appearances were rather rigidly reinforced through dress, it rather underestimates the sheer sexiness of the decade, later reconstructed in the 1980s. This was, after all, also the era of rock 'n' roll and the rise of Elvis-the-Pelvis Presley whose quiffed, suited and then sweat-leathered looks led not only to media hysteria as a thousand wet dreams came true, but also to the whole redefinition of men and masculinity as *the* sexy and looked-at gender. This notion was derived in many ways from the USA, which had also stormed the media and the UK with 'over-paid' and 'over-sexed' GIs in figure-hugging uniforms as well as floods of Hollywood idols. In addition, it was not a lot later that the Mods reinvented the sharp-suited looks of the 1950s and clashed with the Rockers' reconstruction of the frock coat.

However, politically, the 1960s did see a radical discontinuity with previous developments. This primarily came from a whole series of minority, and not so minority, movements: feminism, youth and student protests, peace campaigners, gay groups, civil rights, rising tensions around racism and, in particular, hippie culture which was also welded to the rise of youth culture and 'sex, drugs and rock 'n' roll'. Hippie culture was far and away the most influential of all the movements, as it was the most loosely focused and encompassed most groups and issues: free love, self-expression and spirituality were woolly concepts that could incorporate pacifism, youthism, homosexuality and even some forms of androgynous feminism all at the same time.

The impact of hippie culture on fashion was, as a consequence, immense. Jeans, cheesecloth, velvets, beads, bangles and lengthening hair ultimately, if briefly, became the uniform of almost the entire population under forty. The two or three groups left out, over-forties, stoic conservatives and corporatists, interestingly, were also the praying mantises waiting to take over in the 1980s. The significance of hippie culture upon fashion was, ultimately, threefold. Firstly, it fuelled a near revolution in casual clothing and undermined formal dress as for the middle-class, middle-aged and conservative only; secondly, it created an intense interest in dress and appearance that went hand-in-glove with a rapid increase in mass-produced cheap products and a second-hand market; and thirdly, it led indirectly to the creation of a very strong sense of politically correct dress centred particularly on an anti-middle-class and anti-formal rhetoric. This last factor is tied up with the simultaneous development of identity politics.

Identity politics at their most simple state that identity is not neutral, it is socially shaped and, most importantly, political (Edwards, 1994; Rutherford, 1990; Weeks, 1985). Identity itself is particularly tricky to define other than as a social sense of one's own individuality and location in the wider society, or as the process of self-definition and self-presentation in everyday life. There is an intense sense of conflict here as identity is often seen on the one hand as something of a fixed entity, something one is; whilst it is often equally experienced as contradictory and awkward like an ill-fitting shoe that pinches and slips, or something one may be, could be or would like to become. Identities also tend to multiply and change according to time and place; I am not the same here as there, or the same now as I was.

At the heart of all of this is the tension of the individual and the social, a sense of oneself as the same and yet different to others, as fitting in and as standing out, and as shaped and yet creative. It is, moreover, not surprising that the swirling world of fashion should have so strong a connection with the equally dynamic world of identity, and as the patterns and shapes of the clothes on models turn and mutate in front of us we are also confronted with the three-dimensional kaleidoscope of ourselves: here, now and me. For some, this is taken further to lead to connections to postmodernity and fashion as the epitome of a consumer-oriented, image-driven society where meanings are increasingly less fixed and more chaotic (Baudrillard, 1983; Evans and Thornton, 1989; Kroker and Kroker, 1988).

This current view of identity politics and its relationship to fashion is in many ways new and the result of a collapse in whatever sense of political unity existed previously. To unpack this further necessitates a detailed consideration of some of the unities and tensions concerning dress, appearance and fashion that existed within some of the political groups and movements of the 1960s and 1970s.

Butch, femme or lesbian: fashion and feminism

> Fashion and clothing were seen as constructing and reproducing a version of femininity that was false and constricting and that had to be escaped from or got out of. One way of getting out of the gender identity was to get out of, or to refuse to wear, the fashion and clothing that were constructing that identity. (Barnard, 1996, p. 133)

One of the greatest contributions of second-wave feminism has been the critique of femininity. Femininity – as both the concept and also the associated practices of a special kind of so-called feminine personality of passivity, domesticity and duty to the male of the species – was slammed as either part of the unnecessary trappings of capitalist society or simply the result of centuries of patriarchy and male coercion. Contrary to this lay a rather more complex notion of femininity as repressed or womanhood as undermined (Rich, 1984). It was not entirely surprising, then, that femininity *as appearance* was also attacked as supportive of a male supremacist and/or capitalist empire. If women now saw themselves as not wanting to *act* like the slavish women they were otherwise supposed to, then there was little reason to try to *look* like them either. Therefore, femininity was, in short, seen as wholly *un*natural for women. The practice of this philosophy was, however, never so straightforward and the difficulty lay and still lies in the complex relationships of appearance, personality and practice.

At its simplest, the feminist polemic upon fashion and appearance stated that femininity, in terms of dress and cosmetics manufactured in the name of femininity, was not in any way natural or normal for women. Furthermore, men, rather than women, had been responsible for both producing the goods and inducing women to buy them. Women were, in addition, made to conform to the images prescribed for them by men in both the mass media and the press. Make-up, tight skirts and high heels, for example, were seen as hampering to women who otherwise required hard-wearing and practical, if not necessarily 'masculine', clothing and styles to work and live in, and women did not, of their own volition, want to look 'feminine'. Primary academic examples of opposition to such formations of femininity came from Susan Brownmiller's radical feminist critique of femininity itself as a factor in the social control of women and, more recently, in Naomi Wolf's powerful polemic, *The Beauty Myth*, where the ideals of beauty and the regimes of feminine appearances are seen as the ultimate mechanism in women's oppression as part of a patriarchal postfeminist attempt to reinstate male supremacy (Brownmiller, 1984; Wolf, 1991).

Practical opposition to these constraints came in the form of the now-notorious feminist apparel of the 1970s: cropped hair, no make-up and no jewellery other than politically correct ear-rings, no skirts, lots of trousers and jeans, and a certain penchant for Doctor Martens. Many difficulties with this apparently simple line of thinking were, however, quickly discovered. Firstly, it was difficult to prove that women did not want on some level to look like women, if not traditionally or stereotypically feminine, and that they took no pleasure whatsoever in certain facets of looking attractive or 'feminine' as opposed to 'masculine'. In particular, Janice Winship's, Rachel Bowlby's and, more recently, Hilary Radner's use of psychoanalysis variously asserted that the feminine was neither a fixed nor all-powerful category and that women actively reinvented themselves through its multiple textualities and interpretations (Bowlby, 1993; Radner, 1995; Winship, 1987). This perspective was itself heavily derived from the reinvestigation of the role of psychoanalysis and, more widely, from developments in poststructuralism and cultural studies. Secondly, it was also very difficult to deduce faultlessly that any such desire came simply from early socialization or later mass deception, as this rather implied that women passively soaked up the messages they were given until they equally passively saw the light. In addition, some feminists asserted alternatively that consumption itself formed a site of empowerment for women as an arena of female expertise where men were under-skilled and often excluded (Nava, 1992). Stereotypically, the case of the man shut out from the kitchen, and the common complaint that whilst women may shop effectively for men, men were hopelessly ineffective at shopping for women, formed examples of men's comparative lack of standing in relation to consumption. (Some of these points were clearly overstated as whilst consumption may, on occasions, form a site of empowerment for women this hardly counteracts their exclusion from other sites more related to work or production.) Thirdly, this then led on to a slightly more empirical point of comparison with men, where it was apparent historically and cross-culturally that men have performed highly decorous and impractical roles equal to women, whilst no man of today would claim that a suit and tie is the most practical attire he could think of to wear to work, though he might like to wear these clothes to please himself or to look attractive on some occasions. In addition, men did not all necessarily desire stereotypically feminine women. In sum, these points then rather undermined the claim that there was any simple gender-split in terms of either the desire or the function of clothing or appearance.

Many of these points were discovered over a process of time via women's own experiences or experiments and their attempts to explain their difficulties concerning their appearance theoretically and practically. The present predicament concerns a certain lack of resolution of these inherent tensions: if women do desire some degree of difference from men or some femininity or, more simply, enjoy dressing up as feminine women from time to time, then what is the appropriate form of dress or appearance for women, what is an appropriate form of political action against the pressures to conform to stereotypes of femininity, and where, oh where, does one draw the line? It also started to add up to a dichotomy of fashion as expression versus fashion as oppression, similar in kind to the pleasure versus danger disputes which developed around women and sexuality, and to which there are similarly no easy solutions (Vance, 1984).

Women today are presented with two opposed, yet dominant, images of themselves as femininity and anti-femininity, and their predicament concerns finding their way between these two extremes of the femme Barbie Doll and the butch Diesel Dyke. As a consequence, women's appearance is often connected to almost existential questions of 'who am I?' or, to put it another way, 'butch, femme and back again'. Not surprisingly, then, women have, on the whole and with some exceptions, tended to fail to come up with successful solutions to these questions – at least for women as a group as opposed to women as individuals. The difficulty lies, despite a quite dazzlingly wide variety of styles and choices, in seeing and dividing forms of clothing into the 'me' and the 'not me', frequently according to the degree of femininity or feminism involved, and selecting them accordingly. There is often quite a high degree of anxiety and difficulty felt in juxtaposing styles or recognizing that different looks suit equally different aspects of personality. In short, there is a concern that any *one* appearance *is* personality – that the clothes maketh the woman most completely. This in turn partly depends upon the still all-too-prevalent judgement of a woman's worth through her appearance – something which is increasingly happening to men as well, but which has yet to attain the same overwhelming dominance of their gender.

Where men are concerned, the choices are often simpler and the difficulty frequently lies in the infuriating *lack* of variety. As a result, men's inventiveness is often, of necessity, greater in finding some form of individuality in a sea of convention. This may also explain the apparent and recent rise in male anorexia and eating disorders, as men are increasingly dazzled by the confusion of knowing how to look which has stifled women for the past century at least.

This makes an important point concerning fashion and femininity as the problem for women is often seen in terms of the enforced and fixed nature of femininity, when a far greater difficulty lies in the confusion and anxiety created by the high-speed turnover and diversity of the world of fashion for women. To put it more simply, men on the whole know all too well how to look whilst women do not know well enough.

Underneath all of this, though, is an increasingly fixed regime of physicality, often conducted in the name of health, that affects the sexes similarly if not equally. This involves the role of dieting and exercise for women and the issue of muscularity and strength for men. If there is an increasing variety of styles and accessories sold to the sexes then there is an equally increasing diversity of physical controls. Whilst women are increasingly coerced into slimness, men are increasingly coerced into muscularity. The simple equation in each case is that slimness or muscularity equals success, sexiness and attractiveness. Whilst the perception of dieting is often tempered with concerns relating to the dangers of eating disorders, the emphasis on muscularity, despite the scares over steroids, still shields wider questioning of its other functions or effects. This ultimately also leads to a situation where all other variations are seen as potentially diseased, as slimness and muscularity are also meant to imply healthiness. This is, of course, partially false, as intense dieting and or weight-training are frequently ineffective, if not harmful, forms of exercise. If unwise, though, the relentless pressure upon personalities and bodies continues (Dutton, 1995; Goldstein, 1994; Scott and Morgan, 1993).

If feminism has formed a major critique of femininity and the consumption of fashion, it has also launched an assault on the production of fashion. Fashion remains one of the most contradictory phenomena of contemporary consumer society in its dual aspects of high speed and high spend with no pay and no end to the exploitation of women, and represents the epitome of apparently postindustrial consumption and also the nadir of the most outdated forms of production (Leopold, 1992). One of the reasons for this situation is that the technology of fashion has hardly altered since Singer patented the sewing machine and, in fact, the relentless drive towards expansion and shorter and shorter runs in production has led to a forcing down of working conditions and the insidious incorporation of another factor of production, racial exploitation. Annie Phizacklea in *Unpacking the Fashion Industry* (1990) argues forcefully that the fashion industry could not have survived without the increasing use of Third World skills and materials, and the employment of ethnic minorities in western societies in conditions worse than the lowest white worker would tolerate. Put more concretely, the fashion industry, in lacking an increase in technology, has survived through an equivalent decrease in working conditions for its women and minority workers. (Conversely, technology has advanced in factors of consumption: telemarketing, direct mail, and EPOS (electronic point of sale) information have created faster and more effective ways of selling products, some with deleterious consequences for the customers in terms of surveillance, with no reciprocal pay-off for the fashion industry.)

In sum, then, feminism has provided a powerful critique of femininity and the consumption of fashion (although this has led to some confusion concerning the direction in which to go next), and an equally strong attack on the production of fashion for its ruthless exploitation of women workers and racial minorities. Feminism has not, however, formed a critique of masculinity and fashion, something that was left up to gay men, as outsiders to some forms and aspects of masculinity, to take up and explore.

Drag, camp and macho: gay men and fashion

If feminism provided a powerful critique of femininity and fashion for women, then it was up to gay men as 'outsider men' to provide a similar set of insights into masculinity and fashion for men. These insights were distinctly mixed and heavily derived from the historical position of male homosexuality. Male homosexuality was, and to some still is, seen as almost synonymous with effeminacy: limp-wristed, lisping and dressy queens of high, and low, culture. This conception of homosexuality as masculinity 'in crisis' has a very long, if very varied, history starting with Greco-Roman and Muslim notions of passivity, developing through the molly-houses of the seventeenth and eighteenth centuries, and culminating in the very definition of homosexuality itself in the late nineteenth century as an 'inversion' or a 'feminine soul in a male body' (Bray, 1982; Edwards, 1994; Eglinton, 1971; Tapinç, 1992; Weeks, 1977).

The problematic relationship of homosexuality to masculinity and the part myth/part reality of effeminacy, although mixed up and undermined in various ways throughout the centuries, has never quite been severed. As a result, it was not entirely surprising that those asserting the positivity of gay culture from the late 1960s onwards should also assault the association of homosexuality with effeminacy. The difficulty lay, and still lies, in which way to shove it: a camp masquerade of self-parody typified in drag where effeminacy is pushed all the way into attempted femininity, or an attempt to prove once and for all that gay men are real men too, if not more so.

This latter position, on occasions, led to a sending-up of masculinity itself as the 'hyper' masculinity of clone culture, where leather biker jackets were slung across naked and muscled torsos or skin-tight white T-shirts, whilst button-fly Levis clung to well-defined and accentuated cocks and asses that practically screamed sexual availability. This ended up as something bordering on self-parody (Bersani, 1988; Blachford, 1981; Gough, 1989). The problem undermining this, though, was the very welding of masculinity to sexuality, on occasions literally, as the gay clone was not only the epitome of the appearance of masculinity, he was the epitome of masculine sexuality in concept and practice (Edwards, 1990, 1994). Quentin Crisp's dreams and desires for a 'dark man' were hardly dead, rather they were extolled and expanded upon as the muscular clone in cock-hugging jeans was precisely what many gay men desired and dreamed of and, what is more, this figure now cruised the streets inviting partners to revel in lookalike sex (Crisp, 1968; Lee, 1978; Rechy, 1977).

The difficulty in interpreting the degree of seriousness or silliness involved in all of this led to a series of unresolved discussions throughout the 1970s and the 1980s. For some, this intense masculinization of gay culture represented a triumph of sexual expression and political opposition to heterosexual ideology, whilst for others it meant attempted conformity to oppressive stereotypes of sexual attractiveness and practice. The difficulty lay partly in the interpretation of appearances as, for some, the macho gay clone was precisely a clone, an android, and not a 'real man' at all, only a man who *looked like* a man, hence the constant jokes concerning muscular men in leather jackets discussing cookery and Jane Austen (Bristow, 1989)!

The drag queens and effeminists, meanwhile, had lost out almost altogether. The advent of AIDS had also done little to challenge gay male imagery, if not worsen it in terms of a dreariness of clones without hair, sun-tans, moustaches, muscles and accentuated cocks: in short, clones without sex. However, drag queens regained significant attention in the late 1980s when the Vogue Movement was highlighted in the media. The Vogue Movement referred to an underground network of posing and impressionist dancers taking place in New York and some other major cities where young, gay and often black men would don the costumes and appearances of many cult icons, including Hollywood idols and some, more contemporary, hegemonic images of femininity and masculinity. These were then paraded in front of audiences on the street or in bars and nightclubs, as if in a fashion show, and often set to music as part of a particular contest or competition. The men were otherwise deeply oppressed as outsiders racially, sexually or simply in terms of their effeminacy and poverty, and the practice of voguing partly parodied and partly affirmed the aspirational dreams of the famous magazine and, in particular, their desire for the front cover.

Moreover, the matter of voguing gained media-wide attention and controversy when Madonna, herself an icon of pastiche and parody, released 'Vogue', a highly successful single and an even better video featuring black men dressed in 1940s suits voguing to the record whilst Madonna herself imitated a collection of cultural icons from Bette Davis to Marilyn Monroe via a series of stylized 'front cover' poses. This then spread, diluted, into discoland where dancers desperately tried to pull off the same effect with a series of hand-on-head dance routines. Controversy concerned whether the wealthy Madonna had exploited an oppressed minority movement or given it the media attention it deserved, as much of the original message was lost in a sea of hand gestures (Kellner, 1995; Patton, 1993; Schwichtenberg, 1993).

The potential of the Vogue Movement remains partially untapped, as an adherence to the parody and display of cultural icons has not generally led to an equal parody of the traditional styles of masculinity. This was particularly apparent in the 1980s when the proliferation of images of maleness – from naked torsos and Levi's 501s to 1950s iconography and pinstripe suits – was wide open to parody and take-off. However, there is some evidence for the idea that the impact of this movement has supplemented the slightly increasing diversity of styles displayed in the gay male community, which now include more sporting, work-related and design-led fashions in addition to the perpetual proliferation of fetish, leather and clone looks. As a consequence, the 1980s effected some continuity and change in the gay community's relations with fashion as the intense masculinization of gay culture finally gave way to some variations in style. Interestingly, drag has taken off again in the 1990s through the cult hit movies *The Adventures of Priscilla, Queen of the Desert* and *To Wong Fu, Thanks for Everything, Julie Newmar* and the current style situation represents a jostling sense of change and stasis.

Subcultural style

Dick Hebdige's highly influential, if problematic, analysis of subcultural style in *Subculture: The Meaning of Style* (1979) provided the basis for an analysis of fashion itself as a political phenomenon. He attempted a semi-semiotic analysis of style and its significance for subcultures and, in particular, punk, asserting that it disrupts dominant codes of communication, understanding and commonsense:

> Style in subculture is, then, pregnant with significance. Its transformations go 'against nature', interrupting the process of 'normalisation'. As such, they are gestures, movements towards a speech which offends the 'silent majority', which challenges the principle of unity and cohesion, which contradicts the myth of consensus. (Hebdige, 1979, p. 18)

His work followed heavily on the heels of Stan Cohen, Stuart Hall and Paul Willis, all of whom attempted essentially Althusserian analyses of various phenomena under the auspices of the new deviancy theory (Cohen, 1972; Hall and Jefferson, 1976; Willis, 1977). Consequently, teddy boys and Bowie-ites were seen as reacting equally against the dominant culture and against a society which structurally subordinates them in relation to economic position, unemployment, housing and so on. In a sense, all of these style cultures were then seen as 'noise' or 'interference' in the semiotics of a dominant culture that ultimately incorporated these movements into the culture as a whole on two levels: firstly, through the commodification of subcultural signs into mass-produced objects as, for example, in punk safety-pins seen on the catwalk; and secondly, through the labelling and social control of subcultural activities as 'deviant' via the state and the media. The immediate difficulty with this lies in the assumption of a division of 'dominant' ideology or culture from 'subordinate' ideology or subculture, further problematized by the dominant culture's implied one-way control of its subcultures, when it could be argued that the reality is both more fragmented, less hegemonic and also more mutually influential.

Interestingly, the fashion system itself was seen as central in incorporating outsider or street styles into the mainstream forms of dress and appearance. In particular, the likes of Mary Quant, Zandra Rhodes and even Vivienne Westwood were seen as hijacking street culture and, in particular, punk for haute couture. Punk itself was seen as the epitome of style in revolt, or 'revolting style', against dominant culture. However, the teddy boys' transformation of Edwardian style is seen as a more subtle subversion or 'bricolage' of the original image:

> More subtly, the conventional insignia of the business world – the suit, collar and tie, short hair, etc. – were stripped of their original connotations – efficiency, ambition, compliance with authority – and transformed into 'empty' fetishes, objects to be desired, fondled and valued in their own right. (Hebdige, 1979, pp. 104–5).

Hebdige did, then, also acknowledge the variation in degrees of resistance and conservatism in the styles involved. However, he never escaped the sense of separation, if not divorce, of dominant culture from subordinate or subculture. More problematic still was his constant interpretation of style according to class, as the suit, for example, was automatically equated with conservatism, when in concept and practice its meaning is more varied; and coupled with this there is a serious neglect of gender in defining meaning (see Chapter One). For example, in considering skinheads, he states: 'The boots, braces and cropped hair were only considered appropriate and hence meaningful because they communicated the desired qualities: "hardness, masculinity and working-classness"' (Hebdige, 1979, p. 114). This is, however, precisely the problem with such imagery: its ambiguity. Whilst skinheads reacted violently and successfully against middle-classness, their aggressive acts and looks gave away a profound conservatism, if not reactionary hostility, in terms of masculinity. The skinheads epitomized masculinity untamed and untainted, and consequently found many sado-masochistic admirers in the gay community and fascist sympathizers in the wider society. Similarly, punk, whilst effectively utterly chaotic and confrontational, often reinforced traditional definitions of masculinity in tight, cock-hugging jeans, jerking of phallic guitars, and glorification of nearly all forms of aggression.

This gender dimension was addressed in Angela McRobbie and Mica Nava's *Gender and Generation* (1984), something of a misnomer for a feminist collection of essays that provided a successful critique of femininity yet failed to fully address masculinity or gender more generally – later addressed more successfully in McRobbie's *Zoot Suits and Second-Hand Dresses* (1989). This second collection also raised the significant factor of racial and ethnic variation in the use and interpretation of street style and fashion. From the Zooties of the 1940s in their dressed-for-success suits and the pinstripe hipsters of the 1950s to the later revival of Rastafarianism and dreadlocked reggae culture in the 1970s and 1980s, and even the current crusade of techno-rappers, racial and ethnic minorities have had a long, varied and influential history of association with fashion.

This history has, however, tended to suffer serious neglect in the face of the white, western fashion system.

Afro-Caribbean and Indian, as well as Oriental styles and designs, have been ruthlessly plundered and played out upon the catwalk without acknowledgement; and portrayed as weird, exotic and primitive when they are acknowledged. Kobena Mercer and Isaac Julien have, separately and together, provided detailed critiques of both the representation of racial variation and of stereotypes of black masculinity as potent and primeval, primarily summed up in Robert Mapplethorpe's homoerotic photographic exploration of black masculinity via various displays of enormous cocks (Mercer and Julien, 1988). The fact that the fashion industry brutally exploits the Third World in selling its otherness as exotica or pornography, in stealing its customs and designs, and in exploiting its labour and skills, is well known and easily acknowledged. What is less well understood and consequently significant is the fact that it gets away with it in a way that even Barclays Bank could not in South Africa. The contemporary debate about Naomi Campbell's well-publicized squabbles with the world of supermodels, where she accused agencies of racism in not hiring her because she was black, is a case in point. Being black for the fashion industry means no more than being tall or short, blonde or dark, or a 34B and, in this sense, the fashion system is quite insidiously asocial. The analysis of fashion and racism, then, tends to reflect the concentration of the expression of race within music and style cultures – often without paying equal attention to its connections with wider, or even international, society other than in economic terms (Phizacklea, 1990). The key question of the role of racial and ethnic minorities in exploiting and undercutting dominant styles, for example in voguing, and in turn the wider exploitation of their own particular cultures and styles through mass culture and high fashion, remains wide open to interpretation and often unanswered (however, see Hebdige, 1987).

In his most recent analysis of style cultures entitled *Street Style: From Sidewalk to Catwalk* (1994), published to accompany the Street Style exhibition at the Victoria and Albert Museum in London, Ted Polhemus points to the contemporary tendency to plunder the fashions of the past in faster and faster succession as a 'supermarket of style' where one is a Mod one day, a Punk the next and a raver in the evening with an equal sense of parody and authenticity in each case. This perspective, he asserts, also ties up with the theory and practice of postmodernity. Yet the difficulty with this is that, whilst style cultures have proliferated, they have yet to infiltrate wider society and remain rather confined to students, unemployed youth and disco dancers, whilst bankers continue to go to work in double-breasted suits and everybody wears jeans at the weekend. The end result of this is that street style is tending to plunder and parody itself rather than anyone else.

Consuming passions: meanings, myths and the gay male consumer

One factor curiously lacking in the preceding analysis of the politics of fashion is the question of the role of consumption itself. Fashion requires consumption – spending – in order to display. The role of the gay community, and particularly the gay male community, in relation to consumption and fashion is a particularly important example. Of particular significance is the fact that fashion and dress form a primary means of forming, asserting and displaying an identity. The gay community is unusual in this respect as sexuality, unlike gender or many aspects of race and ethnicity, is not visually recognized without the props of appearance, dress or demeanour (Dyer, 1992). Therefore, expressing oneself gains added significance for the gay community as a visual and potentially political act as well as a personal statement.

Over recent years, a series of stereotypes and myths have developed concerning the role of the gay community in relation to consumption. The most important and pervasive of these is the idea that gay men – as individuals or in groups or childless couples – earn the same or more than straight men with wives and children to support, and therefore have much more discretionary income to spend on themselves, or as they please, as opposed to on necessities. The professionally employed gay male couple has attracted particular attention in this respect and yet there are clearly very marked difficulties in making such claims, not least one of methodology. As homosexuality remains a stigmatized identity open to and unprotected from discrimination, there are clear difficulties in constructing surveys or research which directly address the question of the relationship of sexual orientation and consumption. The primary exception are surveys conducted through the gay press or similar networks where the clear limitation is that the sample is formed from a minority, namely an openly scene-using part of the gay community, which excludes the majority of gay men. In addition, all samples are inherently unrepresentative as the population itself is unknown – there is no electoral roll, household survey or census that covers sexual orientation. On consideration of only some of the difficulties of conducting studies into sexual orientation and consumption it is quite staggering, then, that so much is so often concluded from so little.

A second consideration centres on the lack of recognition of the diversity of the gay community. The assumption that all gay men are white, middle-class and high-earning professionals with few financial commitments is clearly a false perception, stemming at least partly from the distortion which comes from the visibility of some parts of the gay community, often those who are young, affluent and professional, and the invisibility of others, often those who are older, poorer or rurally located. A linked factor here is that high-earning, childless couples are equally often straight, as opposed to gay, and to assume that gay men do not have financial commitments from their primary or secondary families is empirically incorrect. Perhaps most importantly, however, whatever status professional, affluent or middle-class gay men may attain, it remains open to discrimination and is effectively very insecure. Contentiously, and a little less clearly, it is also asserted in some circles that the myth of the affluent gay male consumer is sometimes used to support the Conservative suppression of civil rights on the pretext that the gay male community is comparatively *un*oppressed. Nevertheless, what *is* clear here is that a certain sector of the gay male community which *is* professional and which *can* openly support its sexual orientation through consumption *without* fear of discrimination is of primary importance, past and present, in understanding the relationships of sexuality, masculinity and consumer society.

Of associated importance is the perception of the gay male community as one of trendsetters or, in marketing terms, innovators. One suspects strongly, once again, that whilst certain sectors of the gay male community are first in the queue for some new products, particularly in the consumption of fashion goods, this hardly applies to the entire community or the entire range of commodities. For example, whilst gay men probably were the first to go to work in high-buttoning, single-breasted suits, there are no guarantees that they figure significantly as first-time buyers of Bird's Eye's latest frozen chicken Kiev! The reasons for this development would appear twofold: firstly, as already stated, appearance has an added importance for the gay community in terms of the formation and expression of its identity; and secondly, gay men, in not trying to live up to the ideals and stereotypes of heterosexual masculinity which still include a disdain for dandyism, are more open to the impact fashion marketing may have upon them. Also important in this, though, is the role of gay men in producing style and fashion as designers or magazine editors and, more generally, as an important and productive segment of the image industries.

More recently, some sectors of the gay community, particularly in the USA, have started to assert the potential power of the pink economy to improve the political position of the gay community. This is seen, moreover, to work essentially on three levels: firstly it is asserted that gay commerce forms an increasingly important market in itself and in competition with similar markets; secondly, that the infiltration and promotion of some lesbians and gay men in major corporations is seen to influence policy decisions inside and outside of the organizations concerned; and thirdly, that all lesbians and gay men have the power to boycott or support commercial enterprises and political organizations through the cash register and the ballot box respectively. Impressive as these arguments may at first seem, the transformation of fairly limited economic power into widespread political power is a lot more complex. Few companies which have successfully targeted a gay market have developed or supported anti-discriminatory practices or legislation, at least outside of their own employment policies. Similarly, boycotts, whilst unhelpful, are unlikely to cripple most concerns whose markets are far wider than those explicitly or implicitly developed around the gay community. There is little reason to assume that, if a company provides products or services suited to the gay community, it necessarily supports the gay community politically – selling the product or service remains a sufficient end in itself in most cases.

Similar questions have arisen in the UK, where Europe's first gay-oriented shopping mall along Californian lines has recently opened in Manchester. Whilst its promoters insist on the importance of its development as a safe space for gays to shop, free from comments on their spending patterns or funny looks at the Clinique counter, the sense of seizing economic opportunity with little reference to the politics of sexual equality is never very far away (Aitkenhead, 1996).

Conspicuous by their absence in this discussion, though, are lesbians. Lesbians are often assumed to be the second-rate consumers of the gay community due to the economic discrimination they face as women as well as lesbians. The clear problem here is that being lesbian and being a woman, like being gay and being a man, are inseparable; and the lesbian is a type of woman in a particular and ambiguous position often similar to the gay man whose position is equally ambiguous in relation to men in general. As a result, gay men do not often have the same economic standing or privileges as straight men; and lesbians, conversely, are more likely to work full-time with fewer financial commitments than their heterosexual counterparts. As a result, a recent Channel 4 survey, the results of which were shown on *OUT* in 1994, confirmed that whilst lesbians did earn on average 10 per cent less than their gay male counterparts, they earned up to a third more (on average) than their heterosexual female equivalents. In other words, the economic gender differential between lesbians and gay men is considerably less than that between heterosexual men and women. It is important not to overstate this point for all the reasons already mentioned in relation to the gay community more generally, but it would appear that the notion of the impoverished and oppressed lesbian is as mythical, or as meaningful, as the stereotype of the high-spending guppy.

What all of this tends to add up to is a clear targeting of affluent and secure gay male consumers, equally clear in their lifestyle consequences and purchasing preferences. The primary importance of this is to form the foundation for marketing policies around sexual orientation, and not to set light to the gunpowder of political revolution.

The politics of looking, masculinity and men's fashion

> More recently there has been a blurring of the conventional distinctions in the advertising address to men and women; constructions of masculinity and femininity are less fixed; shopping and self-adornment have become less gendered – less specifically female – activities. (Nava, 1992, p. 166)

The politics of masculinity and men's fashion have traditionally related to men's position over women, their class, status or economic position, and their sexual orientation. In relation to men's fashion itself, many of these distinctions are increasingly less clear-cut and, it is asserted, in design and advertising in the 1980s they were effectively rendered redundant through aggressively self-conscious marketing across these distinctions (Mort, 1988, 1996; Nixon, 1992, 1993; Simpson, 1994, 1996). In particular, the iconography of the sexy, half-naked and muscled man clad only in figure-hugging 501s was derived directly from gay culture of the 1970s; whilst the rise of independent outlets selling higher-quality designer-styled clothing, including Next in particular, marked a direct attempt to undermine class distinctions centred on income and to replace these with a set of distinctions centred on consumption, style, or where you shopped.

On top of this, though, various authors have raised an added question concerning the role or significance of men looking at other men, particularly in terms of consumption (Mort, 1996; Nixon, 1993; Simpson, 1996). The point, put simply, is that in the process of encouraging men to look at other men as consumers of style, fashion and visual display, as opposed to producers of work and achievement, the distinction of heterosexual and homosexual is undermined as, historically, looking at other men is seen as the sole preserve of homosexuals. Most analysis of this process has developed out of 'Mulveyesque' media studies and the question of gendered looking relations discussed previously in Chapter Three; or, more recently, from cultural and literary studies where, in particular, Eve Kosofsky Sedgwick's concept of homosociality and the poststructural reinterpretation of social space have provided primitive tools with which to start to analyse the processes of men looking at other men and their impact upon masculinity (Sedgwick, 1985, 1990, 1993). There are two clear difficulties here, however. Firstly, due to the poststructural drift of the discussion, there is a lack of consideration of underlying mechanisms and, in particular, the role of the media and image industries and the opening up of new markets centred on the consumption of masculine styles. Secondly, these practices are often confined to high-spending, young, gay, racial or city-centred cultures which, in turn, have a long history of association with counter-cultural style practices.

The key question, then, centres on the spread or spillage of such processes of looking into more mainstream practices around style and masculinity. There is clearly a sense in which *all* men are now increasingly encouraged to consider themselves and other men as consumers in visual and style cultures. However, this affects men very differently according to such factors as age, class, race, geography and sexual orientation. Whilst a young, affluent or gay male living in London may feel thrilled at the sense of overspill, others may feel alarmed, defensive, turned off, or left out.

Constantly lurking under the surface of these discussions is the question of sexual orientation. Thus, the real significance of Sedgwick's conception of homosociality its that it puts a finger on the uneasy and messy question of inter-male relations, particularly those relations which are neither defined through work or production nor solely sexual (Sedgwick, 1985, 1990). It is, further, the *extension* of the figure of the cruising gay man, always looking with silent and secret intent, that stands out as significant here; that is, just what *does* happen when men otherwise defined as heterosexual *do* look at other men as visual commodities? For example, to walk into the office and say 'Hey, that's a great suit, where did you get that?' teeters dangerously close to 'Hey, you look great in that suit, do you want a date?'. Whilst, for women, admiring other women's appearances is often perceived as perfectly normal, at least within limits, this strong sense of homosexual jitters that still pervades most inter-male relationships tends to undermine the development of similar practices among men.

Thus, the difficulty of this perspective is that it is all too easy to drastically overstate the case. Whilst it is true to say that the boundaries between gay and straight, or even between male and female, are becoming more blurred in terms of media representations, marketing of up-market fashion and the consumption patterns of some affluent and professional groups, this hardly marks a sea change in the entire population where the categories of male and female, straight and gay, black and white, remain remarkably stable. What all this does amount to is an increasingly clear target marketing of affluent, professional, consumers whether they be black or white, gay or straight, men or women. Whilst there remains a potential for this to spill over into sexual or racial politics, it is still clearly a quantum leap to make from market to polity. More particularly, many of these points rest upon an essentially poststructural assumption or notion of consumption or consumer culture as separate from economics or production, which remains contentious (Featherstone, 1991; Keat, 1994; Lury, 1996). For example, Mort's 'complex tangle of alliances' emphasizes the importance of particular key individuals such as Ray Petri or George Davies in shaping the new consumer masculinity, yet misses the sense in which these actors themselves were the products of wider social, economic and political developments around consumerism (Mort, 1996, p. 113).

The position of men's fashion in relation to women was, and still is, harder to define, yet the increasing attention to men's fashion – through everything from advertising to designer collections and style magazines – has at least started to undermine the fundamental gender differences in terms of fashion. Fashion is no longer simply feminine in terms of consumption and masculine in terms of production, as more men now consume it and more women produce it or directly influence it as designers or retailers. The difficulty here, though, is that the market for women's fashion still drowns out the equivalent market for men several times over. The relation of male ethnic minorities to men's fashion, meanwhile, has not moved significantly out of its location within music and dance cultures. As a result, the impact and politics of masculinity and men's fashion remain mixed and uncertain.

Conclusions: the politics of dressing up

This chapter has started to unpack the sexual, racial and gendered implications of, in particular, men's fashion. This has shown that there is a very strong sense in which all fashion is a highly political phenomenon. At the start of this chapter, though, I asserted that fashion was widely seen as an *apolitical* phenomenon and there is a sense in which this is still correct. Fashion is, perhaps uniquely, free from overt forms of political constraint. There are significantly few laws, regulations or rules relating to fashion and yet our appearances are deeply located within an unwritten series of conventions on how to look: the politics of dressing up. In particular, there are no laws governing what we should wear to work, to the theatre or to take part in other formal or informal activities and yet we all somehow and very expertly know how to look: that a pinstripe suit is appropriate for the City, an interview or a formal dinner and jeans are equally fitting for shopping, washing the car or sitting around.

The question raised is only partly one of how we know, as this is clearly a process of imitation and picking up cues; it is, more to the point, a question of *why* we continue to stick to such conventions so meticulously and with so little sense of compromise. For example, the power of street cultures to shock and upset the applecart of appearances lies precisely in the very fixed nature of conventions of style and fashion themselves. Despite the apparent plethora and ephemerality of all the ways one *could* look, the question of *how* to look is heavily constrained in contextual dependencies that act like a set of chains on the potent opportunities that dressing up offers for self-expression and, ultimately, social change. The capacity to develop and change depends on the fact that we never get it quite right, that we make mistakes, and that in doing so consistently we turn the tide in the sea of conventions. The politics of dressing up, whether related to identity or not, represent a conscious attempt to force the issue further and to make these mistakes correct; yet as these opportunities continue to open up, new constraints develop to control the outcomes, and this forms the focus of the final chapter.

8

The Sting in the Tale:
Social Policy and Social Divisions

The contemporary expansion in men's fashion, in concept and practice, is popularly perceived as a positive development in undermining traditional sexual divisions and/or opening up new sources of self-expression or pleasure for men themselves (Hix, 1984; Spillane, 1993; York and Jennings, 1995). Moreover, academic attention to this issue has lent some credence to these notions, seeing men's fashion as a catalyst for a new sexual politics, at least potentially, or as starting to pull apart traditional conceptions of masculinity (Mort, 1986, 1996; Nixon, 1992, 1993; Simpson, 1994, 1996).[1] In this final chapter, I wish to question the perception of the expansion of men's fashion and interest in their appearance as an unequivocally positive development, on two levels: in relation to the pitfalls of consumer society and the social policy applied to it; and more specifically, in connection with its impact upon masculinities and men themselves. Whilst I do not wish to overthrow the more positive aspects of contemporary developments in men's fashion and masculinity entirely, I do wish to provide a strong sense of their limits.

Social policy and consumer society

Social policy has not had a history of association with the world of fashion, and yet there are many connections between social policy and the experience of shopping, spending on fashion and the politics of consumption. More importantly, as consumption increases in its importance, so social, economic and even criminal policy or legislation is developed to shape its outcomes (Cahill, 1994).

This is not an entirely new series of processes or developments. Sumptuary laws, for example, were used to control the perceived extravagance of the middle classes, particularly in the wake of Puritanism in pre-modern, mercantile capitalism.[2] There is some continuity in this as the current use of VAT in the UK is applied to goods seen as 'luxury', including stationery, information technology, electrical goods, alcohol, cigarettes and tobacco, cars and petrol, and adult clothes. The recent controversy concerning VAT on fuel and other proposed areas, including children's clothes and newspapers, arose from the perceived necessity of these goods.

It could be argued, however, that in an increasingly consumer-led society – and one which enjoys a consistently higher, if unequal, standard of living – these distinctions are increasingly redundant. In particular, as the majority of people now own a car and use it, increasingly, as a necessity to get to work, the continual and relentless increases on fuel, road tax and car prices are hard to justify and governments have had to turn to ecological rather than economic excuses. Equally, taxes on alcohol and tobacco derive as much support from health and morality campaigns as from any sense of economic fairness, as the population as a whole has easy and frequent access to alcohol and, in fact, the working classes are more likely to smoke.

It is immediately clear, then, that social policy applied to consumption is far from neutral or value-free. It is, in fact, a growing and increasingly controversial area of concern that strikes at the very core of our values and morals as well as our senses of equality and freedom. It is the primary purpose of this section, then, to expose these issues as present, yet often implicit, within consumer-related policy, and to apply this, where appropriate, to the world of fashion, which represents the epitome of consumer society. I also want to start to address the social divisions arising out of consumption and, indeed, perpetuated and reinforced through social policy. Particularly significantly, I want to look at how this then links into questions of masculinity, and the social divisions that are developing not so much across genders as within them.

Social policy and shopping

Social policy as applied to shopping has three primary areas of impact: firstly, on pricing, through taxation and related costs; secondly, on spending, through tax on income and supplementary provision of credit; and thirdly, on crime – mainly shoplifting and debt collection. Allied concerns also include trades descriptions and the regulation of advertising, the growing awareness of shopping addiction as a social problem, and the impact of consumer lobby groups. All of these areas then have their specific applications to the world of fashion.

Social policy and pricing

The primary aspect of social policy affecting pricing in the UK is, of course, VAT. (Similar tax measures are often operated in other nations and the commentary here is relevant internationally, at least in general terms.) VAT (Value Added Tax) is technically an indirect tax – that is one which is paid indirectly via the purchase of goods and not directly from personal income – and also a tax which is widely seen as regressive or non-distributing of income and wealth, as the poorest pay most as a proportion of their income. This is an important point to make, as one of the justifications for constant increases in the rates of VAT is that it is only applied to luxury or inessential goods. But VAT is applied to many goods and services which we would now consider rudimentary, if not essential, such as many electrical goods or, in particular, clothing; and the distinction of the essential from the inessential is socially and personally relative. For example, an expansive array of expensive fashions is extravagant for a nurse yet expected for many of those working in advertising, marketing or media industries.

The VAT levied on adult clothing is particularly anachronistic, as whilst fashion may be a luxury, clothing itself is quite clearly essential and related to survival in a similar way to food. No distinction is made to determine clothing from fashion, other than in children's clothing (which invokes notions of protection, correct parenting and even infanticide if a child is not dressed appropriately). I suspect that the justification for the taxation on clothing comes from the same ideology that underlay sumptuary laws. Thus, the conception of expenditure on clothing as conspicuous consumption or the equation of fashion and extravagance is still strong in our culture today.

The rate of VAT is currently 17.5 per cent in the UK, more than twice what it was when the Conservative government first came to power in 1979. The recent furore over VAT on fuel highlighted the growing perception of the tax as an anachronistic and socially divisive lining of central government's purses, which hits the poorest and most socially disadvantaged hardest and does little to provide the services that these groups need. Additional duty taxes are levied on alcohol, tobacco and some imported fashion goods, perhaps more fairly, though with the same degree of moral censure implicit in the policy.

Social policy and spending

The traditional impact of social policy on spending comes, once again, in the form of taxation, though this time directly through income tax. The impact of income tax on spending is, at first sight, common-sensical and clear: the more one is taxed, the less one spends and vice versa in an apparently direct inverse correlation of taxation and spending. The immediate difficulty of this equation is that the factors affecting spending are far more complex. They include personal wealth, employment position, demography, interest rates (affecting housing and savings), exchange rates (affecting travel and the value of sterling), inflation, economic growth and recession, and, not least, the psychology of spending or the much discussed 'feel-good factor'.

Income tax is, technically, a progressive tax, in the sense that it is proportional and the poorest pay less or least. However, in the UK, massive cuts in the top rates of income tax mean they are now less than 60 per cent of what they were fifteen years ago; and rises in value-added and regressive taxation compensate for lower basic rates of income tax. In addition, economic recession traditionally hits areas such as expenditure on fashion hardest and, in particular, expenditure on men's fashion. One would assume then, that spending on such goods has fallen significantly, but in fact it has increased.[3]

A key factor in this increase is the rise of multiple means of payment and, in particular, credit. The use of credit in the 1980s accelerated to unprecedented levels through the opening up of a whole series of financial markets and, in particular, the development of store cards or in-store credit. At its peak, over one third of all purchases were made on plastic (Cahill, 1994). Of particular importance in this trend were department stores, electrical stores and high-street fashion outlets, who developed a dazzling array of credit options. It is now the case that many major high-street retailers offer and actively promote their own credit cards, frequently offering discounts, competitions and other offers with which to lure in the unsuspecting customer, often at point-of-sale. Many of these developments (including the expansion of shopping malls and supermarkets covered in Chapter Six) are essentially 'imports' from the USA where they are 'nothing new'; whilst the development of these practices in other parts of Europe, particularly Southern Europe, is far more limited.

Coupled with this development was the expansion of mail order into previously unexposed up-market areas. Mail order since the Second World War had formed one of the central means of gaining credit for clothing and household goods with few questions asked, and was often achieved via extensive use of warehouse clearance of poorer-quality merchandise. Its success was also centred on certain demographic factors and, in particular, the preponderance of working- and lower-middle-class wives with time on their hands, little money and a network of other women living in similar positions with whom they could use the catalogues to gain friends. The difficulty with these early forms of mail-order agency catalogue systems, though, was not only the often inferior quality of the goods, or even the 'cheap and nasty' series of associations that developed around them, rather it was the rise of working women themselves for whom such purchasing was seen as inappropriate – they had less time, more money and required more up-market, stylish goods that were easily ordered, quickly received and did not involve anyone else. Into this network of needs entered the Next Directory, a hard-backed, glossy catalogue offering a range of mid- to up-market styles for the affluent working woman, or man, with a local rate 'phone call, forty-eight-hour delivery, and a personal account only if needed. The higher prices were easily justified and the Directory was, despite a problematic period in the late 1980s, a runaway success story. Other companies have since followed suit as Harrods and Selfridges stores run their own mail-order service and new outlets such as Cotton Traders, Lands End and Racing Green have developed mail-order markets for the more affluent consumer.

Optimistic though many of these developments may seem in providing customers with more options, the underlying reality is a good deal less rosy. At the centre of the increasing controversy surrounding such developments is the phenomenal rise in debt. The easy availability of credit combined with the very high numbers of incentives in every form (from advertising and discounts to interest-free accounts) has led to considerable numbers of people getting into serious debt. The individual is often blamed for their apparent stupidity in not seeing the long-term problems coming, but the responsibility ultimately lies not with the retailers themselves, whose non-stop luring in of the customers is in part understandable, but with the lack of government-led regulation of accountability. Today, it is perfectly possible to wander from shop to shop opening a credit account in each one – subject only to a confirmatory phone call to ascertain credit status – promptly gaining the facility to spend hundreds and thousands of pounds in total, in addition to any credit cards one may already have. One can proceed to open an equally vast array of mail-order accounts, entitling one to more spending. The only thing stopping this process, therefore, is the will-power of the person concerned; that is, until the monthly statements start to land on the doormat.

Access to credit now forms one of the main forms of social division in contemporary society, and taps into our deepest concerns with civil liberties and personal and social responsibility. Generally speaking, anyone with a secure (though not necessarily permanent) income from full-time work, who falls within the limits of socially appropriate consumption in having a permanent home address and a perceived capacity to pay (in terms of income not spent on housing or other loans), with no record of serious credit default, can gain credit from anywhere at any time. Those not in full-time employment, without a fixed address, or with records of credit default, cannot. Records of credit default work retrospectively, that is they are set in place once the consumer is already in serious arrears. In addition, computerized records are increasingly kept on an individual's credit status and are used to regulate future transactions and access to facilities, and to target promotional activities. This quite clearly divides the affluent, often white, and working population from the unemployed, casually or part-time employed, students, minors, the elderly, the ill, homeless or temporary residents and non-working women. This second group, whilst potentially the poorest payers, are often the most in need of at least minimal credit. This also accounts for the tendency of such groups to fall into the trap of using loan sharks, or private lenders, who often use extortionate rates of interest and threatening tactics to operate effectively.

The difficulty with nearly all forms of credit is the interest charges that accrue on any uncleared sum. These vary, yet are often extortionately high, running at rates in excess of 20 and even 30 per cent per annum in the UK. Store cards often operate at the highest rates whilst credit cards operate at somewhat lower rates, some under 20 per cent per annum; and banks often offer the cheapest rates on loans and overdrafts, though in all cases rates are likely to exceed 10 to 15 per cent p.a. calculated on a daily rate. As a consequence, as access to credit has increased, so has default on credit payments.

Credit default is generally dealt with on a case-by-case basis and by debt counsellors such as those employed by the Citizens Advice Bureaux. They seek to assist the client by drawing up lists of outgoing and incoming monies and sharing out all income unused on essentials to all creditors, proportionately. Most creditors will freeze interest and accept some form of reduced monthly payment, provided payments are kept up without default and credit facilities are, quite literally, cut. The difficulties tend to concern banks, who are frequently hostile to freezing interest rates, require added securities and are more likely to threaten and harass the customer into paying up, particularly if levels of credit are high. If creditors do refuse to freeze interest or continue to make excessive demands on the customer, there are few courses of action which the customer can take and few sources of support. One recent development is the formation of Credit Unions, state-funded agencies which provide credit on lower interest terms. The problem remains the slippery slope of any form of credit, as it is exceedingly difficult to clear deficits when they accrue to high levels, without significant income injections, increased cash flow or circumstantial support. Credit in fact forms the ultimate poverty trap as, once difficulties set in, there is a strong tendency to spiral downwards into poverty. When all else fails, the final recourse is to repossession of all forms of property and to bankruptcy.

These pitfalls concerning consumption and credit are gradually gaining recognition as social – and not merely individual or idiosyncratic – issues. Nevertheless, to truly redress the situation would require a curtailing of some forms of individual freedom and access to spending as one pleases, or perhaps the use of more vociferous means-testing in controlling credit levels. However, such measures remain potentially more divisive and deeply unpopular, perhaps understandably, with both the public and the government. Difficulties concerning access to credit, credit default and escalating poverty continue to increase, though, with some even more deleterious consequences.

Social policy and consumer crime

Consumer crime essentially takes two forms: shoplifting or theft; and credit default leading to criminal prosecution. The production and promotion of goods and services are also subject to certain forms of legislative regulation and protection.

Shoplifting is now a recognized crime as well as a semi-recognized mental illness in the form of kleptomania. These two elements of crime and illness account for the often contradictory reaction to shoplifting: perception of it as a costly social problem and as an individual and psychological phenomenon. The former perspective has proved most influential in justifying incorporation of shoplifting costs into price policies. There is a tendency to exaggerate its significance here (as is the case with industrial action), though the effect on the consumer is often neglected. The second perspective has fuelled populist feminist rhetoric concerning the psychological effects of isolation and housewifery. Neither of these perspectives is entirely correct, as the majority of shoplifting is by staff. This is hardly surprising given the increasing prevalence of high-tech security and surveillance devices in many high-street stores, which severely restrict the customer's, rather than the staff's, opportunities for theft. However, concern is also raised as to the stigmatizing effects of prosecution for shoplifting on those customers who either make mistakes or are psychologically ill.

Similar issues concern so-called shopaholicism or shopping addiction, where customers shop to fulfil deep-seated psychological or social needs in a similar way to other forms of addiction such as alcoholism or drug dependency. There is a certain pop-psychological foundation to such allegations as well as a strong North American influence in the highlighting of its social effects and the categorization of individual cases. Even so, the preponderance of clothing and fashion in shoplifting and shopaholicism is of interest. Whilst some of this is explained in terms of convenience, as a shirt is easier to steal than a computer (and this similarly applies to self-service supermarkets where shoplifting has long been built into overhead costs) the greater explanation lies in the cultural value of the goods concerned (see for example, Doe, 1996).

Clothing and fashion accessories clearly fulfil psychosexual needs in ways that a can of paint or a packet of salt cannot. In addition, the promotional activities surrounding such goods are more prevalent, and are premised more upon their social and personal worth to the individual than their utility value. Clothing and fashion have long histories of marketing according to association: a new outfit as a new you, a new perfume for a new sensation, and a new look for a whole new, successful, sexy and high status profile: in short, the commodification of personality.

It is this factor which, I would suggest, accounts for the significance of shoplifting and shopaholicism in stores catering for fashion goods, whether on the part of staff, who are in the promotional world of the store all day long, or on the part of the consumer, who is seduced into the shop through a series of insidious self-presentations that act like mirrors to those who think of themselves as assertive and confident as well as to those who feel confused, frustrated or dislocated in their lives.

The second area of consumer crime, credit default, is often dealt with successfully in a highly individualized way, as outlined earlier. However, on occasions, further measures come into force. The Consumer Credit Act of 1974, the Trades Descriptions Act of 1968 and the Consumer Protection Act of 1987 all seek to provide the consumer with some protection from psychosexual or financial exploitation in the name of profit – whether in terms of hard sells, misrepresentation of goods or poor after-sales service. The difficulty lies, though, in the fact that making a claim lies entirely in the hands of the individual who must try to take on increasingly monopolized retailing giants. The credit default register or blacklist is compiled according to serious allegations of non-payment or refusal to pay on the part of the customer, and it is up to the company or creditor concerned to report the customer. The customer is not necessarily informed effectively of their blacklisting, and access to information is severely restricted. An individual can apply to clear their name, yet will need to clear all outstanding debts and show evidence of a significantly improved financial position (in terms of employment for example). For the vast majority of those who fall on to the register, this is unattainable. Unemployment, along with the breakup of a personal or family relationship and the illness or death of an economically active party, in fact form the main causes of serious debt. This raises issues concerning credit, debt and poverty as symptoms rather than causes of major social and economic problems.

Social policy and social divisions

Consumer society is often presented as the epitome of opportunity for all – an 'open shop'. From the preceding discussion, this is quite clearly empirically limited if not entirely mythical. Consumer society does indeed offer many opportunities for pleasure, for self-expression and for self-fulfilment for those who can afford it and for those who have access to it. It is apparent, then, that when we talk of the opiate pleasures of consumption, we are primarily referring to a select group of affluent consumers, well-located in economic and geographical terms, with the transport, time and money to shop for luxury goods. (Even they still face the dreary trudge around the supermarket.) This then excludes many or all of the elderly, the poor, the unemployed, those without their own transport, single parents, the infirm, or those with minimal discretionary income. These groups are likely neither to afford nor have full access to the opportunities and pleasures of consumer society.

All of this tends to mean the reconstruction of new social divisions, often centred on older, traditional divisions of class, race, age and gender. The decidedly piecemeal state of social policy in taxing the poorest hardest, creating difficulties in gaining credit, stigmatizing shoplifting and offering every incentive to everyone else, merely adds to the sense of the same social divisions. This is a quite insidious situation and one which lacks critical academic or political attention, with some exceptions. It is partially explained as the outcome of the expansion of poststructural theory and cultural studies around consumption, which seek primarily to divorce consumption from any economic or empirical foundation and assert instead its semi-autonomous state as a separate sphere of activity or culture (Featherstone, 1991; Keat, 1994; Lury, 1996). Whilst such approaches highlight the significance of cultural phenomena for those incorporated within its parameters, this similarly excludes consideration of the rest and reinforces academically the same sense of social divisions. Thus, whilst there is clearly a need for the insights of such studies, there is also a need to redress the emphasis.

Of key interest in this text is the interconnection of gender and consumption. Apart from the point mentioned previously concerning the perception of the consumer primarily as feminine, there are clearly secondary connections with other forms of social divisions, as it was historically the white, young and middle-class woman who was the primary pawn in the game of consumption. Similarly, as men's involvement in all aspects of consumerism has increased, including personal, fashion and lifestyle related forms of consumption, so predominantly white, middle-class and young men, as the most affluent, are increasingly seen as targets for marketers, advertisers and producers alike. This tends to exclude older, working-class and non-white men, with the exception of non-white professionals or young working-class men living at home with high discretionary incomes. In sum, this amounts to the reinforcement through consumption of social divisions according to class, race and age *within* the genders as much as, or more than, across them. To make this clearer, I wish to examine the example of men's fashion.

Fashion, masculinity and consumer society

Fashion is often seen as the epitome of consumer society, as an extravagant waste of resources and the primary example of the semiotic rather than practical value of commodities (Evans and Thornton, 1989; Farschou,

1988; Kroker and Kroker, 1988). This is juxtaposed in postmodern contradiction with the notion of fashion as the nadir of archaic, industrial exploitation (Phizacklea, 1990). In each case the common association is with fashion's importance for women as consumer victims or as a producer underclass. Masculinity as a site of association and consequence for fashion is unquestioned, but it is quite clear that there are indeed questions to answer. For if fashion is increasing in its importance for men, if men now spend more time shopping and also shop more for themselves, and if men now constitute the growth gender market, then the impact of these developments upon masculinity must surely rank as significant.

The key question is, of course, *if* these developments are, in fact, taking place. Certain empirical points of reference would seem important. Many men now spend less time working, whether in terms of lower working hours or through unemployment, whilst the situation for women has reversed and their time spent working has increased. Men are also targeted as consumers in ways that they were not previously, through advertising, magazines and new product and service areas varying from moisturizers to designer fashion. Developments in extended opening hours and out-of-town or city-located shopping malls, meanwhile, favour the employed and car-owning male consumer. Masculinity as traditionally defined in relation to aspects of physicality, muscularity, appearance and sexuality is wide open to inducements of anxiety and commodified solutions to it – from multi-gyms to leather jackets. And finally, men (as far and away the wealthier gender) are worth tempting – a gold mine for producers, retailers and marketers alike. The potential of the consequences of these developments, therefore, is immense. The problem remains the contemporary nature of many of these processes, which are still mutating as I write. It is, in short, too soon to know. However, it is worthwhile finding out, if the mistakes of the past, practised primarily upon women, are not to repeat themselves this time upon men.

These mistakes were comprised of several elements: the assertion that consumption reinforced (rather than undermined) traditional notions of femininity; that this then led to the setting up of a hierarchy of socially approved forms of femininity or womanhood, where the overweight woman in particular was castigated as a pariah and the thin woman held up as an aspiration; and most controversially, that this then drove women into psychological illness – from depression, anxiety and low self-esteem, to anorexia and other eating disorders, and even the disasters of plastic surgery (Wolf, 1991). Whilst the chain of causality or logic in this is increasingly seen as less clear-cut, involving more individual and psychological factors, the sense of the (re)creation of a hierarchy of femininities through consumption remains prevalent and of importance.

Whilst I do not wish to fuel feminist fires of controversy concerning the significance of these issues for women, I do wish to raise the significance of these issues for men. Most importantly, despite the proliferation of the multiple representations of masculinity, from the waifs of Britpop to the muscularity of *Baywatch*, the content of these images and representations remains fixed, divisive and hierarchical, particularly in relation to questions of age, colour and weight. The positive or valorized images of masculinity remain, despite variations, primarily young and white, slim and trim; whilst the vilification of men without muscle tone or flat stomachs has increased. As a consequence, then, it is not merely affluent men who have most to gain from the expansion of consumption, in terms of self pleasures or social validation, it is young, trim and white men with intrinsic good looks. As a result, consumer society often offers the old, fat, ugly or 'socially crippled' man little except increasing castigation for his non-conformity.

The difficulty here is that the chain of causation for men is, in all likelihood, as complex as that for women, and to assume that this drives *all* men into dieting and fitness is clearly off target. Yet what remains is an increasing sense of anxiety concerning the imagery and indeed sexuality of masculinity, and a clear concern that at least *some* men are made to feel anxious or to take action in relation to how they look. In particular, the popularity of weight training among many young men, the rise of image consultancies for men, and their increased expenditure on their appearance – from designer fashions and moisturizers to suntans and plastic surgery – is evidence of this, and is not explained, though often justified, as fitness. If fitness were the sole aim, men would run more, eat healthily and go swimming, not swing weights, get sun-tans and face-lifts!

As a result of all of this, a hierarchy of masculinities is emerging according to image and appearance, where young white men with pumped-up pecs, strong jaw-lines and flat stomachs rule over the rest with a phallocentric intensity. In relation to men's fashion, it is this sense of social division at the level of physical appearance which appears of paramount importance, and which also reinforces wider hierarchies of masculinity according to age, class and race as well as the position to consume. In sum, whilst the white, young, trim and good-looking man with plenty of income and the means to spend it has much to gain from the pleasures and passions of the expansion of fashion in tandem with consumer society, the older, less affluent, less fit or more rurally located man faces an increasing onslaught of negative comments and criticism for his failure to live up to an ideal type. Consumer society may well open up opportunities for some, yet it slams doors in the faces of others.

Conclusions: the sting in the tale

This chapter has formed the sting in the tail of this text, in the sense that it has raised serious questions concerning the negative consequences of what is otherwise often seen as a positive set of developments in men's fashion and masculinity.

Social policy, as applied to consumer society, is piecemeal and complex, showing a strong similarity to the history of social policy in the UK more generally. The decades following the Second World War and, in particular, the last fifteen or twenty years have also seen an essentially unchecked and unregulated growth in consumerism. Moreover, though, the formal deregulation of financial markets in the 1980s, the significant expansion of credit, and the use of regressive taxation policies have also led to a series of serious social and economic difficulties for some groups concerning credit default, poverty, dependency and economic exploitation. In addition, this has led to a series of social divisions according to access, credit status and the position to consume. In this sense, fashion is quite seriously regulated and controlled. All this then constructs a hierarchy of masculinities on two levels: according to physical appearance, youth, colour and slimness; and according to wider social divisions including class, age, geography and race. The one exception to this situation is the issue of sexual orientation, as gay and straight sexuality are increasingly confused in a world that eroticizes and commodifies certain forms of masculinity, although this is easily overstated (see Chapter Seven).

It still remains the case, however, that women are perceived as the primary victims of these processes. Yet, as male unemployment and poverty levels continue to rise in tandem with the increasing targeting of affluent men as consumers, there is some tentative evidence to suggest that this situation is changing, and the personal and social risks facing men as consumers have increased to unprecedented levels. It is too soon to know the full outcome of these developments. What is important, however, is that the lessons and mistakes of the past, in terms of individual addiction, social division and economic poverty, are learned and not repeated. This requires proactive intervention sooner not later. The time has already come for men, and society, to look into the mirror.

Notes

1. Chapman and Rutherford's edited collection is something of an exception here as a more critical and feminist-driven set of perspectives on the development of the New Man.

2. See Chapter One and Chapter Two for further evidence on this point.

3. See particularly Chapter Four here, plus Key Note and Mintel reports.

Conclusion: Men's Fashion, Masculinity and Consumer Society

> Men – gays, bisexuals and 'straights' – are now as much a part of modern consumerism as women. Their construction of a sense of who they are, of their identity as men, is now achieved as much through style of dress and body care, image, the right 'look', as women's. This process of identity construction and maintenance among men need not necessarily displace a sense of identity derived from the world of work; in some cases it may be combined with such a source of identity. Nevertheless, there is an increasing number of men who now define themselves through their patterns of consumption rather than through a work-role identity. Work provides money for purchasing the consumer goods required to construct and maintain an identity. For the unemployed some may construct a sense of identity through the limited amount of consumption of music, clothing, eating and drinking patterns which they are able to afford, while others become unable to sustain an adequate sense of identity without a work role and without the money that provided the means for sustaining an identity through patterns of consumption. (Bocock, 1993, p. 105)

When writing of men's fashion, masculinity and consumer society, one is confronted with two opposed images of men. One is of an affluent, often young, slightly narcissistic and certainly self-conscious man of uncertain sexual orientation; the other is of a man often older, with a family and with little time, money or interest to invest in his appearance. These two representations are partly stereotypes and yet, like all stereotypes, they contain a grain of truth.

The determining factors that differentiate these two images are gender and consumption, and this explains why this text in considering men's fashion has had, of necessity, to consider masculinity and consumer society. For what separates these two examples is their construction of masculinity – around appearances in the first instance, or around family and work roles in the second; and their economic and demographic positions – affluent, youthful and often financially uncommitted in the first case, or older, married and deeply monetarily committed in the second.

I do not raise these distinctions idly, as they underpin the central points of this entire text. Firstly, men's fashion needs understanding sociologically as part of wider processes in masculinity and consumer society, and not as an elitist and design-driven cultural practice. Secondly, the current expansion of interest in the concept and practice of men's fashion, from designer styles to moisturizing lotions, is only partly explained as the outcome of developments in sexual politics (in particular, the impact of second-wave feminism). It is explained more fully as the result of wider processes in consumer society – most importantly, the increasing social significance of patterns of consumption, self-presentation and lifestyle as constitutive of identity. Thirdly, in asserting the interlocked significance of gender issues and consumption in understanding men's fashion, a series of interconnected social divisions is enacted around each of these axioms where wealthy, good-looking and well-located young men are increasingly socially valorized over older, uglier or poorer men.

This also constructs a complex hierarchy of masculinities according to economics, demography and appearances. For some, one more positive consequence of this is that these patterns start to undermine other more traditional divisions among men centred upon work roles, ownership or, more complexly, sexual orientation.[1] At the crux of this, though, is a questioning of a certain democratic ideal, or the idea that any man can take part in these consumption-oriented activities or enjoy style and fashion regardless of his prior position.[2] It also taps into what one might call the ideology of the look, the notion that any man can look a certain way. Any man quite clearly can*not* look a certain way as he is constrained by his fiscal and physical limits. Importantly, men do not partake in consumer society equally according to such factors as age, physique, location, income and financial commitments. Underpinning this discussion is the cultural influence of the United States where social or even physical constraint is often unacknowledged and rampant individualism is a way of life – as in the example of cosmetic surgery, which is now seen in some areas of California as the logical extension of changing one's clothes. The one and only limit here is money.

This analysis started with a consideration of classical and historical perspectives on the development of men's fashion. These perspectives were criticized as often too elitist in their focus on haute couture, or insufficiently gendered in their analysis. In particular, fashion remained an essentially unquestioned and feminine phenomenon. The rise of the New Man in the wake of second-wave feminist analyses of gender started to address seriously the issue of masculinity in relation to the perceived expansion of interest in men's fashion. However, this tended to miss the underlying significance of wider economic and demographic factors, including marketing, in reconstructing a masculinity centred on consumption. The marketing of men's fashion itself was used to show how masculinity was increasingly commodified and marketed in the 1980s, and a case study was provided of the success of the Next chain of stores in this respect. It was also demonstrated that men's style magazines, which formed a growth market in themselves, were used to stimulate demand for products and set up a rhetoric of correctness concerning men's style and appearances. This market- or production-driven analysis was then compared with the empirical experience of consumers themselves. More significantly, the potential of fashion to provide a source of oppositional support for oppressed groups was considered, particularly in relation to identity politics and the role of the gay male consumer. Ultimately, though, it was pointed out that expansion of interest in men's fashion (and its attendant emphasis on appearances) was a more limited and socially divisive development, which tended to affect men differently and unequally, according to such factors as age, class, race, or sexual orientation.

This opens up a further question, though, of the more specific effects of these processes on the people concerned. Clearly, those with the looks, the income and the time on their side have never had it so good, in terms of the opportunities which the expansion of men's style and fashion have to offer them. These are pleasures indeed: deeply sensual, sexual and auto-erotic indulgences where consuming new costumes, their colours, details and sensations, as well as their looks and poses, is as delicious as eating expensive ice-cream. But those without the luck, the looks or the time have never had it so bad, and are consigned to looking and longing, or even exclusion and castigation for not playing the game. In this sense, fashion is fascism: conform in the mirror of judgements or else take the consequences.

It is this other, darker side of fashion, unseen around corners and in crowds, that is left out of so many of the more contemporary and classical analyses of men's fashion.[3] Men are indeed in the mirror – not only in terms of their own narcissism, but in terms of a mirror that the world around them is holding up to scrutinize their appearances. In this sense, masculinity is indeed in crisis, yet not from the scrutiny of sexual politics, more from the market: dress for success and dress to kill, indeed.

This darker side of fashion contrasts sharply with the more popular perception of its lightness, its fun, and its frivolity. Fashion does offer the opportunity for quick, easy and often inexpensive transformations of personality or presentation of self. For example, the simple dismantling of a dull suit and tie and the adoption of cheerfully coloured T-shirt and soft jeans can transform the mood and look of a tired office worker; whilst the stunning array of styles and designs now found in high-street stores clearly offers many men the opportunity to express themselves and to *enjoy* themselves. But this is still not the whole story, and what we are left with is a contradictory sense of fashion as social control versus fashion as self-expression.

This sense of opposition or contradiction that underpins men's fashion taps into a wider set of meanings. Fashion is full of contradictions: active yet structured, individual yet social, meaningful yet meaningless, changing yet static, endlessly produced yet endlessly consumed. Ultimately, this accounts for its sociological significance; it also goes some way to explain its fascination, its irritation and perhaps even its passion. It also perhaps explains why, despite the expansion of style and fashion for men and women, so many people dress so dismally or poorly with no sense of style or fashion at all (Gill, 1995). When thinking of men and fashion, though, this does not explain the sense of unease that still surrounds the truly stylish or fashion-conscious man. The historic equation of fashion with the feminine remains unanswered and unbroken. Like Pandora's box, fashion remains uncontainable and inexplicable, and once opened up into all its wild and chaotic colours it can never be closed, once felt it is never lost, once started, never stopped and, like the Sphinx, you can never solve its endless riddles.

Notes

1. See Mort, 1986, 1996; Nixon, 1992, 1993; Simpson, 1994, 1996 particularly.

2. I should point out here that the inspiration for this point came from an interview I conducted with the late editor of GQ magazine in the UK, Michael VerMeulen, himself an American committed to the democratic ideals of men's consumption of style and their own masculinity. I have some sympathy with his project – why should men not enjoy consuming their own masculinity? I do not, moreover, wish to criticize a man who cannot now correct me. I merely wish to expose the underlying ideology of his position and of many others like him.

3. More feminist analyses are, however, often ambivalent concerning the role of fashion. See, for example, Chapman and Rutherford, 1988; Craik, 1994; Wilson, 1985.

Epilogue

> Behind the dialectic of voyeurism-exhibitionism in everyday self-presentations are the high emotional costs of appropriated desire and commodified selfhood that are constituted as signs of a consumption-based ideology in which the destruction of the subject is all but completed. (Langman, 1992, pp. 73–4)

During the writing of this book I read, or rather attempted to read, the novel by Bret Easton Ellis called *American Psycho* (1991). The book tells the tale of Patrick Bateman, a highly successful dealer on Wall Street, who is also intelligent, charming and stunningly good-looking. He occupies his spare time working out, watching videos or wining and dining with his colleagues. They discuss accounts or deals and, more significantly, ask Patrick's advice on shopping and on the etiquette of men's dress, design and the correct style and accessories – from knots in ties to the crease in trousers. He also delivers the details of what everyone wears, at regular intervals, and discusses with the reader the right way to shave and moisturize, the products to use, and the technical specification of his CD player. He gives a full description of the contents of his closets, which consist of dozens of designer suits, shirts, ties and accessories, even including his very expensive socks and shoes.

What drives the novel along is the insight one gains into his other activities. He routinely castigates, often attacks and occasionally kills people living on the streets, because he has a loathing of their messy and sometimes smelly appearances. His own front-cover model appearances attract numerous female and some male admirers. The homosexual men he is contemptuous of, and he murders them mercilessly. The women he scrutinizes for perfection, routinely seduces, performs a series of perverse sexual acts with or on, and then frequently tortures, mutilates and ultimately kills, sometimes over a period of several days, keeping parts of their anatomy for further experiments. This excites him, often to orgasm. He is a psychopath.

Radical feminists in North America were outraged at the apparent attempt to provide a guide to the serial rape and murder of women. Apart from the fact that some of his victims were men, this missed the point that it was not so much Patrick who was pathological – although this was certainly the case – rather it was the society that produced him and (for the most part) let him get away with it. That society, needless to say, is a consumer society and, whilst very extreme, Patrick's activities represent the final outcome of a society that values monetary worth over human life, that commodifies personality to the point of its extinction, and takes a concern with appearances to its ultimate amoral, apocalyptic and genocidal end.

Several months later, when I was on a leisurely trip to Covent Garden in London with a friend, we decided to take a look around some of the most up-market and designer-oriented stores for fun. Having a love of clothes and fashion, I expected to enjoy it, yet as we wandered around the shelves in the stylized stores, I gained a growing sense of something sinister at work in the condescending looks of store assistants, the parading and near-cruising of the clientele, conspicuously carrying their designer goods and rifling through the rails. I felt under-dressed (ridiculous, as I was to all intents and purposes *well* dressed) and ultimately *un*dressed, stripped of any dignity, as I was merely considered for the commodities I wore, as first one and then another set of eyes roved over me. I wasn't attacked and I certainly wasn't dead; yet I felt for all the world that, like a black shadow, Patrick Bateman had just brushed by me.

References

Adorno, T. and Horkheimer, M. (1993) 'The Culture Industry: Enlightenment as Mass Deception', in S. During (ed.) *The Cultural Studies Reader*. London: Routledge.

Aitkenhead, D. (1996) 'No sniggering, no staring, no pretence', *Independent Weekend*, 3 February, p. 4.

Amiel, B. (1994) 'I wear funny clothes, therefore I am', *Independent*, 29 May.

Amies, H. (1994) *The Englishman's Suit: A Personal View of its History, its Place in the World Today, its Future and the Accessories Which Support it*. London: Quartet.

Armstrong, S. (1996) 'Catch 'em young', *Sunday Times*, Culture Supplement, 12 May, p. 10.

Ash, J. (1989) 'Tarting up Men: Menswear and Gender Dynamics', in J. Attfield and P. Kirkham (eds) *A View from the Interior: Feminism, Women and Design*. London: The Women's Press.

Ash, J. and Wright, L. (eds) (1988) *Components of Dress: Design, Manufacturing and Image-Making in the Fashion Industry*. London: Routledge.

Ash, J. and Wilson, E. (eds) (1992) *Chic Thrills: A Fashion Reader*. London: Pandora.

Attfield, J. and Kirkham, P. (eds) (1989) *A View from the Interior: Feminism, Women and Design*. London: The Women's Press.

Baldwin, F. E. (1926) *Sumptuary Legislation and Personal Regulation in England*. Baltimore, MD: Johns Hopkins.

Barnard, M. (1996) *Fashion as Communication*. London: Routledge.

Barnes, R. and Eicher, J. B. (eds) (1992) *Dress and Gender: Making and Meaning in Cultural Contexts*. Oxford: Berg.

Barthel, D. (1992) 'When Men Put on Appearances: Advertising and the Social Construction of Masculinity', in S. Craig (ed.) *Men, Masculinity and the Media*. London: Sage.

Barthes, R. (1985) *The Fashion System*. London: Jonathan Cape.

Batterberry, M. and Batterberry, A. (1982) *Fashion: The Mirror of History*. London: Columbus (2nd edn).

Baudrillard, J. (1981) *For a Critique of the Political Economy of the Sign*. St Louis, MI: Telos Press.

Baudrillard, J. (1983) *Simulations*. New York: Semiotext(e).

Bauman, Z. (1992) *Intimations of Postmodernity*. London: Routledge.

Bell, D. and Valentine, G. (eds) (1995) *Mapping Desire: Geographies of Sexuality*. London: Routledge.

Benjamin, W. (1982) *Illuminations*. London: Cape.

Berger, M. (*et al.*) (eds) (1995) *Constructing Masculinity*. New York: Routledge.

Bersani, L. (1988) 'Is the Rectum a Grave?', in D. Crimp (ed.) *AIDS: Cultural Analysis, Cultural Activism*. London: MIT Press.

Blachford, G. (1981) 'Male Dominance and the Gay World', in K. Plummer (ed.) *The Making of the Modern Homosexual*. London: Hutchinson.

Bocock, R. (1993) *Consumption*. London: Routledge.

Bohdanowicz, J. and Clamp, L. (1994) *Fashion Marketing*. London: Routledge.

Bourdieu, P. (1984) *Distinction: A Social Critique of the Judgement of Taste*. London: Routledge & Kegan Paul.

Bourdieu, P. (1993) *Sociology in Question*. London: Sage.

Bowlby, R. (1993) *Shopping with Freud*. London: Routledge.

Brain, R. (1979) *The Decorated Body*. London: Hutchinson.

Bray, A. (1982) *Homosexuality in Medieval and Renaissance England*. London: Gay Men's Press.

Bristow, J. (1989) 'Homophobia/ Misogyny: Sexual Fears, Sexual Definitions', in S. Shepherd and M. Wallis (eds) *Coming On Strong: Gay Politics and Culture*. London: Unwin Hyman.

Brooke, S. (1996) 'The anorexic man', *Sunday Times*, Style Supplement, 11 February, p. 17.

Brown, S. (1995) *Postmodern Marketing*. London: Routledge.

Browning, F. (1994) *The Culture of Desire: Paradox and Perversity in Gay Lives Today*. New York: Vintage Books.

Brownmiller, S. (1984) *Femininity*. New York: Simon & Schuster.

Buchbinder, D. (1994) *Masculinities and Identities*. Melbourne: Melbourne University Press.

Burman, B. and Leventon, M. (1987) 'The Men's Dress Reform Party 1929–37', *Costume*, **21**, pp. 75–87.

Byrde, P. (1979) *The Male Image: Men's Fashion in Britain 1300–1970*. London: Batsford.

Cahill, M. (1994) *The New Social Policy*. Oxford: Blackwell.

Calhoune, C. (*et al.*) (1993) *Bourdieu: Critical Perspectives*. Cambridge: Polity.

Campbell, C. (1992) 'The Desire for the New – Its Nature and Location as Presented in Theories of Fashion and Modern Consumerism', in R. Silverstone and E. Hirsch (eds) *Consuming Technologies: Media and Information in Domestic Spaces*. London: Routledge.

Carrigan, T. (*et al.*) (1985) 'Toward a new sociology of masculinity', *Theory and Society*, **14**, pp. 551–604.

Chapman, R. (1988) 'The Great Pretender: Variations on the New Man Theme', in R. Chapman and J. Rutherford (eds) *Male Order: Unwrapping Masculinity*. London: Lawrence & Wishart.

Chapman, R. and Rutherford, J. (eds) (1988) *Male Order: Unwrapping Masculinity*. London: Lawrence & Wishart.

Chartered Institute of Marketing (1993) *Certificate Fundamentals and Practice of Marketing*. London: BPP Publishing Ltd.

Chenoune, F. (1993) *A History of Men's Fashion*. Paris: Flammarion.

Cohen, S. (1972) *Folk Devils and Moral Panics: The Creation of Mods and Rockers*. London: Martin Robertson.

Connell, R. W. (1987) *Gender and Power: Society, the Person and Sexual Politics*. Cambridge: Polity.

Connell, R. W. (1995) *Masculinities*. Cambridge: Polity.

Cook, D. (1994) 'Shopping and the sex war', *Attitude*, August, pp. 76–9.

Cooper, E. (1995) *Fully Exposed: The Male Nude in Photography*. London: Routledge (2nd edn).

Corrigan, P. (1993) 'The clothes-horse rodeo; or, how the sociology of clothing and fashion throws its (w)reiters', *Theory, Culture and Society*, **10**, pp. 143–55.

Craig, S. (ed.) (1992) *Men, Masculinity and the Media*. London: Sage.

Craik, J. (1994) *The Face of Fashion: Cultural Studies in Fashion*. London: Routledge.

Creekmur, C. and Doty, A. (eds) (1995) *Out in Culture: Gay, Lesbian, and Queer Essays on Popular Culture*. London: Cassell.

Crisp, Q. (1968) *The Naked Civil Servant*. Glasgow: Collins.

Davis, F. (1992) *Fashion, Culture, and Identity*. Chicago: University of Chicago Press.

Doe, T. (1996) 'I shop therefore I am', *Madame Figaro*, March, pp. 30–2.

Driscoll, M. (1995) 'Non-drip gloss for men', *Sunday Times*, 9 April.

During, S. (ed.) (1993) *The Cultural Studies Reader*. London: Routledge.

Dutton, K. R. (1995) *The Perfectible Body: The Western Ideal of Physical Development*. London: Cassell.

Dyer, R. (1985) 'Male Sexuality in the Media', in A. Metcalf and M. Humphries (eds) *The Sexuality of Men*. London: Pluto.

Dyer, R. (1989) 'Don't Look Now', in A. McRobbie (ed.) *Zoot Suits and Second-Hand Dresses: An Anthology of Fashion and Music*. London: Macmillan.

Dyer, R. (1992) *Only Entertainment*. London: Routledge.

Dyer, R. (1993) *The Matter of Images: Essays on Representation*. London: Routledge.

East, R. (1990) *Changing Consumer Behaviour*. London: Cassell.

Edge, S. (1995) 'Consuming in the face of hatred: lifestyle and the gay advance', *Soundings*, 1, 1, pp. 163–74.

Edwards, T. (1990) 'Beyond Sex and Gender: Masculinity, Homosexuality and Social Theory', in J. Hearn and D. Morgan (eds) *Men, Masculinities and Social Theory*. London: Unwin Hyman.

Edwards, T. (1994) *Erotics and Politics: Gay Male Sexuality, Masculinity and Feminism*. London: Routledge.

Eglinton, J. Z. (1971) *Greek Love*. London: Neville Spearman.

Eicher, J. B. (ed.) (1995) *Dress and Ethnicity: Change Across Space and Time*. Oxford: Berg.

Elias, N. (1978) *The Civilizing Process: The History of Manners* (Volume One). Oxford: Blackwell.

Elias, N. (1982) *The Civilizing Process: State Formation and Civilization* (Volume Two). Oxford: Blackwell.

Ellis, B. E. (1991) *American Psycho*. London: Picador.

Emberley, J. (1988) 'The Fashion Apparatus and the Deconstruction of Postmodern Subjectivity', in A. Kroker and M. Kroker (eds) *Body Invaders: Sexuality and the Postmodern Condition*. London: Macmillan.

Evans, C. and Thornton, M. (1989) *Women and Fashion: A New Look*. London: Quartet.

Falconer, K. (1996) 'Orange suits on Savile Row? outrageous', *Independent Weekend*, 18 May, p. 6.

Farren, M. (1985) *The Black Leather Jacket*. New York: Abbeville Press.

Faurschou, G. (1988) 'Fashion and the Cultural Logic of Postmodernity', in A. Kroker and M. Kroker (eds) *Body Invaders: Sexuality and the Postmodern Condition*. London: Macmillan.

Featherstone, M. (1991) *Consumer Culture and Postmodernism*. London: Sage.

Fejes, F. J. (1992) 'Masculinity as Fact: A Review of Empirical Mass Communication Research on Masculinity', in S. Craig (ed.) *Men, Masculinity and the Media*. London: Sage.

Finkelstein, J. (1991) *The Fashioned Self*. London: Polity.

Fiske, J. (1987) *Television Culture*. London: Methuen.

Flugel, J. C. (1930) *The Psychology of Clothes*. London: Hogarth Press.

Flugel, J. C. (1965) 'The Evolution of Garments', in M. E. Roach and J. B. Eicher (eds) *Dress, Adornment and the Social Order*. London: John Wiley.

Frankel, S. (1994) 'Store whores', *Attitude*, August, pp. 79–80.

Friedberg, A. (1993) *Window Shopping: Cinema and the Postmodern*. Oxford: University of California Press.

Gaines, J. (1986) 'White privilege and looking relations: race and gender in feminist film theory', *Cultural Critique*, fall, pp. 59–79.

Gaines, J. and Herzog, C. (eds) (1990) *Fabrications: Costume and the Female Body*. London: Routledge.

Gibbings, S. (1990) *The Tie: Trends and Traditions*. London: Studio Editions.

Giddens, A. (1990) *The Consequences of Modernity*. Cambridge: Polity.

Gill, A. A. (1995) 'The way we wear', *Sunday Times*, Style Supplement, 26 February, p. 6.

Gitlin, T. (1986) 'We Build Excitement', in T. Gitlin (ed.) *Watching Television: A Pantheon Guide to Popular Culture*. New York: Pantheon Books.

Glynn, P. (1978) *In Fashion: Dress in the Twentieth Century*. London: Allen & Unwin.

Goffman, E. (1965) 'Identity Kits', in M. E. Roach and J. B. Eicher (eds) *Dress, Adornment and the Social Order*. London: John Wiley.

Goldstein, L. (ed.) (1994) *The Male Body: Features, Destinies, Exposures*. Ann Arbor: University of Michigan Press.

Goodwin, C. (1996) 'Men on the makeover', *Sunday Times*, Style Supplement, 16 June, pp. 8–9.

Gough, J. (1989) 'Theories of Sexuality and the Masculinization of the Gay Man', in S. Shepherd and M. Wallis (eds) *Coming On Strong: Gay Politics and Culture*. London: Unwin Hyman.

Gray, S. (1995) 'Can the image makers cramp your style?', *Financial Mail*, 29 October, pp. 32–3.

Green, I. (1984) 'Malefunction: a contribution to the debate on masculinity in the cinema', *Screen*, 25, 4–5, pp. 36–48.

Gross, L. (1989) 'Out of the Mainstream: Sexual Minorities and the Mass Media', in E. Seiter (*et al.*) (eds) *Remote Control: Television, Audiences and Cultural Power*. London: Routledge.

Hall, S. and Jefferson, T. (1976) *Resistance through Rituals: Youth Subcultures in Post-War Britain*. London: Routledge.

Hanke, R. (1992) 'Redesigning Men: Hegemonic Masculinity in Transition', in S. Craig (ed.) *Men, Masculinity and the Media*. London: Sage.

Harker, R. (*et al.*) (eds) (1990) *An Introduction to the Work of Pierre Bourdieu: The Practice of Theory*. Basingstoke: Macmillan.

Hart, C. (1994) '"By gum pet, you smell gorgeous": representations of sexuality in perfume advertising', unpublished conference paper.

Harwood, V. (*et al.*) (eds) (1993) *Pleasure Principles: Politics, Sexuality and Ethics*. London: Lawrence & Wishart.

Hebdige, D. (1979) *Subculture: The Meaning of Style*. London: Routledge.

Hebdige, D. (1987) *Cut'n'Mix: Culture, Identity and Caribbean Music*. London: Comedia.

Heller, S. (1993) 'Scholars debunk the Marlboro Man: examining stereotypes of masculinity', *Chronicle of Higher Education*, February, pp. A8–15.

Hix, C. (1984) *Man Alive! Dressing the Free Way*. New York: Simon & Schuster.

Hoch, P. (1979) *White Hero, Black Beast: Racism, Sexism and the Mask of Masculinity*. London: Pluto Press.

Hollander, A. (1988) *Seeing through Clothes*. London: Penguin.

Hollander, A. (1994) *Sex and Suits*. New York: Knopf.

Horsham, M. (1996) 'The Hit Factory', *Arena*, March, pp. 106–10.

Jameson, F. (1984) 'Postmodernism, or the cultural logic of late capitalism', *New Left Review*, 146, pp. 53–93.

Jameson, F. (1988) 'Postmodernism and Consumer Society', in E. A. Kaplan (ed.) *Postmodernism and its Discontents: Theories, Practices*. London: Verso.

Keat, R. (*et al.*) (eds) (1994) *The Authority of the Consumer*. London: Routledge.

Kellner, D. (1995) *Media Culture: Cultural Studies, Identity and the Politics between the Modern and the Postmodern*. London: Routledge.

Key Note Report (1987) *Men's Clothing Retailers*. London: Key Note Publications.

Kidwell, C. B. and Steele, V. (eds) (1989) *Men and Women: Dressing the Part*. Washington: Smithsonian Institution Press.

Kirkham, P. and Thumim, J. (eds) (1993) *You Tarzan: Masculinity, Movies and Men*. London: Lawrence & Wishart.

Kroker, A. and Kroker, M. (1988) *Body Invaders: Sexuality and the Postmodern Condition*. London: Macmillan.

Kunzle, D. (1982) *Fashion and Fetishism: A Social History of the Corset, Tight-Lacing and Other Forms of Body Sculpture in the West*. Totowa, NJ: Rowman & Littlefield.

Langman, L. (1992) 'Neon Cages: Shopping for Subjectivity', in R. Shields (ed.) *Lifestyle Shopping: The Subject of Consumption*. London: Routledge.

Lash, S. (1990) *Sociology of Postmodernism*. London: Routledge.

Laver, J. (1968) *Dandies*. London: Weidenfeld & Nicolson.

Laver, J. (1969) *Modesty in Dress*. Boston, MA: Houghton Mifflin.

Laver, J. (1982) *Costume and Fashion: A Concise History*. London: Thames & Hudson (2nd edn).

Lee, J. A. (1978) *Getting Sex: A New Approach – More Fun, Less Guilt*. Ontario: Mission Book Company.

Lee, M. J. (1993) *Consumer Culture Reborn: The Cultural Politics of Consumption*. London: Routledge.

Lehrer, J. (1989) 'The New Man: that's entertainment!', *Media and Values*, fall, pp. 8–11.

Leopold, E. (1992) 'The Manufacture of the Fashion System', in J. Ash and E. Wilson (eds) *Chic Thrills: A Fashion Reader*. London: Pandora.

Levene, L. (1996) 'One size fashion: an ill-fitting insult to the neglected art of tailoring', *Independent Weekend*, 6 April, p. 4.

Liddle, A. M. (1994) 'Masculinity, social practice and the body', unpublished conference paper.

Lister, D. (1995) 'Dressed to kill, by Italian designers', *Independent*, 21 October.

Lurie, A. (1981) *The Language of Clothes*. London: Heinemann.

Lury, C. (1996) *Consumer Culture*. Cambridge: Polity.

Lyotard, J. F. (1984) *The Postmodern Condition*. Manchester: Manchester University Press.

McCracken, G. (1985) 'The Trickle-down Theory Rehabilitated', in M. Solomon (ed.) *The Psychology of Fashion*. Lexington, MA: Lexington Books.

McCracken, G. (1988) *Culture and Consumption: New Approaches to the Symbolic Character of Consumer Goods and Activities*. Indiana: Indiana University Press.

McDowell, C. (1994) 'Material gains', *Sunday Times*, Style Supplement, 2 October, pp. 4–5.

McKendrick, N. (*et al.*) (1982) *The Birth of a Consumer Society*. London: Europa.

McRobbie, A. (ed.) (1989) *Zoot Suits and Second-Hand Dresses: An Anthology of Fashion and Music*. London: Macmillan.

McRobbie, A. and Nava, M. (eds) (1984) *Gender and Generation*. London: Macmillan.

Margolis, J. (1995) 'Last orders for the New Lad fad', *Sunday Times*, Style Supplement, 23 April, pp. 4–5.

Martin, R. and Koda, H. (1989) *Jocks and Nerds: Men's Style in the Twentieth Century*. New York: Rizzoli.

Mercer, K. and Julien, I. (1988) 'Race, Sexual Politics and Black Masculinity: A Dossier', in R. Chapman and J. Rutherford (eds) *Male Order: Unwrapping*

Masculinity. London: Lawrence & Wishart.

Miller, D. (ed.) (1995) *Acknowledging Consumption: A Review of New Studies*. London: Routledge.

Mintel (1987) *Men's Outerwear*, August, pp. 97–109.

Mintel (1989) *Suits within the Men's Outerwear Market*, June, 7.3–7.24.

Molloy, J. T. (1975) *Dress for Success*. New York: David McKay.

Moore, S. (1988) 'Getting a bit of the Other – The Pimps of Postmodernism', in R. Chapman and J. Rutherford (eds) *Male Order: Unwrapping Masculinity*. London: Lawrence & Wishart.

Mort, F. (1986) 'Image/change: high street style and the New Man', *New Socialist*, November, pp. 6–8.

Mort, F. (1988) 'Boy's Own? Masculinity, Style and Popular Culture', in R. Chapman and J. Rutherford (eds) *Male Order: Unwrapping Masculinity*. London: Lawrence & Wishart.

Mort, F. (1996) *Cultures of Consumption: Masculinities and Social Space in Late Twentieth-Century Britain*. London: Routledge.

Mulvey, L. (1975) 'Visual pleasure and narrative cinema', *Screen*, **16**, 3, pp. 6–18.

Nava, M. (1991) 'Consumerism reconsidered: buying and power', *Cultural Studies*, 5, 2, pp. 157–73.

Nava, M. (1992) *Changing Cultures: Feminism, Youth and Consumerism*. London: Sage.

Neale, S. (1982) 'Images of men', *Screen*, 23, 3–4, pp. 47–53.

Neale, S. (1983) 'Masculinity as spectacle: reflections on men and mainstream cinema', *Screen*, 24, 6, pp. 2–16.

Nixon, S. (1992) 'Have You Got the Look? Masculinities and Shopping Spectacle', in R. Shields (ed.) *Lifestyle Shopping: The Subject of Consumption*. London: Routledge.

Nixon, S. (1993) 'Distinguishing Looks: Masculinities, the Visual and Men's Magazines', in V. Harwood (*et al.*) (eds) (1993) *Pleasure Principles: Politics, Sexuality and Ethics*. London: Lawrence & Wishart.

Oakley, A. (1981) *Subject Women*. London: Fontana.

Pahl, R. (1993) 'What price that old black magic now?', *New Statesman and Society*, February, pp. 31–2.

Patton, C. (1993) 'Embodying Subaltern Memory: Kinesthesia and Problematics of Gender and Race', in C. Schwichtenberg (ed.) (1993) *The Madonna Connection: Representational Politics, Subcultural Identities and Cultural Theory*. Oxford: Westview Press.

Pfeil, F. (1994) *White Guys: Studies in Postmodern Domination and Difference*. London: Verso.

Phizacklea, A. (1990) *Unpacking the Fashion Industry*. London: Routledge.

Polhemus, T. (1994) *Street Style: From Sidewalk to Catwalk*. London: Thames & Hudson.

Pumphrey, M. (1989) 'Why do cowboys wear hats in the bath? Style politics for the older man', *Critical Quarterly*, 31, 3, pp. 78–100.

Radner, H. (1995) *Shopping Around: Feminine Culture and the Pursuit of Pleasure*. London: Routledge.

Randall, G. (1993) *Principles of Marketing*. London: Routledge.

Rechy, J. (1977) *The Sexual Outlaw: A Documentary*. London: W. H. Allen.

Retail Business (1980) *Men's Wear Part 1*, July, 269, pp. 56–60; *Part 2*, August, 270, pp. 45–51; (1983) *Part 1*, October, 308, pp. 26–31; *Part 2*, November, 309, pp. 27–34; (1987) *Part 1*, December, 358, pp. 8–15; (1988) *Part 2*, January, 359, pp. 40–50.

Retail Intelligence (1994) *Clothing Retailing*, 6.

Rich, A. (1984) 'Compulsory heterosexuality and lesbian existence', in A. B. Snitow (*et al.*) (eds) *Desire: The Politics of Sexuality*. London: Virago.

Richards, E. A. and Rachman, D. (eds) (1978) *Market Information and Research in Fashion Management*. Chicago, IL: American Marketing Association.

Roach, M. E. and Eicher, J. B. (eds) (1965) *Dress, Adornment and the Social Order*. London: John Wiley.

Rodowick, D. N. (1982) 'The difficulty of difference', *Wide Angle*, 5, 1, pp. 4–15.

Roper, M. and Tosh, J. (eds) (1991) *Manful Assertions: Masculinities in Britain since 1800*. London: Routledge.

Rowley, J. (1994) '"Making it through the wilderness": teenage girls, sexuality and Madonna', unpublished conference paper.

Rubinstein, R. P. (1995) *Dress Codes: Meanings and Messages in American Culture*. Oxford: Westview Press.

Russell, L. (1994) 'Spend, spend, spend', *Independent Magazine*, 10 December.

Russo, V. (1987) *The Celluloid Closet: Homosexuality in the Movies*. New York: Harper & Row.

Rutherford, J. (1988) 'Who's that Man?', in R. Chapman and J. Rutherford (eds) *Male Order: Unwrapping Masculinity*. London: Lawrence & Wishart.

Rutherford, J. (ed.) (1990) *Identity: Community, Culture, Difference*. London: Lawrence & Wishart.

Scheuring, D. (1988) 'Heavy Duty Denim: "Quality Never Dates"', in A. McRobbie (ed.) *Zoot Suits and Second-Hand Dresses: An Anthology of Fashion and Music*. London: Macmillan.

Schwichtenberg, C. (ed.) (1993) *The Madonna Connection: Representational Politics, Subcultural Identities and Cultural Theory*. Oxford: Westview Press.

Scott, S. and Morgan, D. (eds) (1993) *Body Matters: Essays on the Sociology of the Body*. London: Falmer Press.

Sedgwick, E. K. (1985) *Between Men: English Literature and Male Homosexual Desire*. New York: Columbia Press.

Sedgwick, E. K. (1990) *Epistemology of the Closet*. Berkeley: University of California Press.

Sedgwick, E. K. (1993) *Tendencies*. London: Routledge.

Seiter, E. (*et al.*) (1989) *Remote Control: Television, Audiences, and Cultural Power*. London: Routledge.

Segal, L. (1990) *Slow Motion: Changing Masculinities, Changing Men*. London: Virago.

Shepherd, S. and Wallis, M. (eds) (1989) *Coming On Strong: Gay Politics and Culture*. London: Unwin Hyman.

Shields, R. (1992) *Lifestyle Shopping: The Subject of Consumption*. London: Routledge.

Simmel, G. (1973) 'Fashion', in G. Wills and D. Midgley (eds) *On Individuality and Social Forms*. Chicago, IL: University of Chicago Press.

Simpson, M. (1994) *Male Impersonators: Men Performing Masculinity*. New York: Routledge.

Simpson, M. (1996) *It's a Queer World*. London: Vintage.

Solomon, M. (ed.) (1985) *The Psychology of Fashion*. Lexington, MA: Lexington Books.

Spencer, N. (1992) 'Menswear in the 1980s: Revolt into Conformity', in J. Ash and E. Wilson (eds) *Chic Thrills: A Fashion Reader*. London: Pandora.

Spillane, M. (1993) *Presenting Yourself: A Personal Image Guide for Men*. London: Piatkus.

Staples, R. (1982) *Black Masculinity: The Black Male's Role in American Society*. San Francisco, CA: Black Scholar Press.

Stockbridge, S. (1990) 'Rock Video: Pleasure and Resistance', in M. E. Brown (ed.) *Television and Women's Culture: The Politics of the Popular*. London: Sage.

Strinati, D. (1995) *An Introduction to Theories of Popular Culture*. London: Routledge.

Sudjic, D. (1989) *Cult Heroes: How to be Famous for More than Fifteen Minutes*. London: Andre Deutsch.

Tapinç, H. (1992) 'Masculinity, Femininity, and Turkish Male Homosexuality', in K. Plummer (ed.) *Modern Homosexualities: Fragments of Lesbian and Gay Experience*. London: Routledge.

Tester, K. (ed.) (1994) *The Flâneur*. London: Routledge.

Tomlinson, A. (ed.) (1990) *Consumption, Identity, and Style: Marketing, Meanings, and the Packaging of Pleasure*. London: Routledge.

Triggs, T. (1992) 'Framing Masculinity', in J. Ash and E. Wilson (eds) *Chic Thrills: A Fashion Reader*. London: Pandora.

Vance, C. S. (ed.) (1984) *Pleasure and Danger: Exploring Female Sexuality*. London: Routledge.

Veblen, T. (1925) *The Theory of the Leisure Class: An Economic Study of Institutions*. London: Allen & Unwin.

Warde, A. (1994) 'Consumption, identity formation and uncertainty', *Sociology*, 28, 4, pp. 877–98.

Wark, P. (1996) 'What a man can do to change his image', *Sunday Times*, Style Supplement, 16 June, p. 9.

Weeks, J. (1977) *Coming Out: Homosexual Politics in Britain from the Nineteenth Century to the Present*. London: Quartet.

Weeks, J. (1985) *Sexuality and its Discontents: Meanings, Myths and Modern Sexualities*. London: Routledge.

Welsh, I. (1994) 'Merchandising men or marketing masculinity?', unpublished conference paper.

Wernick, A. (1987) 'From Voyeur to Narcissist: Imaging Men in Contemporary Advertising', in M. Kaufman (ed.) *Beyond Patriarchy: Essays by Men on Pleasure, Power, and Change*. Toronto: Oxford University Press.

Williams, S. (1996) 'A life in the shift of . . .' *Independent Weekend*, 3 February, p. 4.

Williamson, J. (1986) *Consuming Passions: The Dynamics of Popular Culture*. London: Marion Boyars.

Willis, P. (1977) *Learning to Labour: How Working Class Kids Get Working Class Jobs*. Farnborough, Hants: Saxon House.

Wilson, E. (1985) *Adorned in Dreams: Fashion and Modernity*. London: Virago.

Wilson, E. and Taylor, L. (1989) *Through the Looking Glass: A History of Dress from 1860 to the Present Day*. London: BBC Books.

Winship, J. (1987) *Inside Women's Magazines*. London: Pandora Press.

Wolf, N. (1991) *The Beauty Myth: How Images of Beauty are Used Against Women*. London: Vintage.

Yarwood, D. (1992) *Fashion in the Western World 1500–1990*. London: Batsford.

York, P. (1995) 'Nineties, what nineties?', *Arena*, December, pp. 20–2.

York, P. and Jennings, C. (1995) *Peter York's Eighties*. London: BBC Books.

Index